READERS RESPOND TO

NO LONGER A SLUMDOG

"I LOVED your book! Recommended it to many others who are also reading it. So eye-opening and inspirational."
—Ms. T.K., Southern Pines, North Carolina

"These children's stories have captured me."
—Mrs. S.N., Gap, Pennsylvania

"These words you put on paper were obviously inspired from our Father. This book brought tears and 'God bumps' to me throughout my reading. Between you, Francis Chan and David Platt, I am so convicted to do more in the name of Christ."
—Mrs. R.H., Lorain, Ohio

"I was truly blessed by the work God is doing in Asia. You have encouraged me to pray for the children and the work."
—Mr. T.L., Tucson, Arizona

"I got your book today and finished reading it within an hour. As a 17 year old with a passion for helping others, this book broke my heart and gave me hope all at once. Thank you for writing such an inspiring book."
—Ms. C.K., Cambridge, Ohio

"God knew just what I needed—He sent me your book! . . .
Your book has inspired me once again to never stop loving and
to never stop giving. It has expanded my heart for the lost."

—Ms. C.M., Springdale, Arkansas

"*No Longer A Slumdog* was almost impossible to put down."

—Ms. J.C., Ontario, Canada

"I just finished your new book *No Longer a Slumdog*. Wow.
Your words and the stories of these children and their families
brought me tears of sadness at their plight and tears of joy at
what Jesus is doing in India."

—Mr. J.H., College Station, Texas

"This book has been revolutionary to both my husband and me.
We've passed it on, hoping it will do the same for someone else."

—Mrs. D.H., Claremore, Oklahoma

"This is an awesome book, and everyone needs to read it."

—Mr. D.R., Sevierville, Tennessee

"Heartbreaking, eye-opening, and inspiring! This is a beautiful
book and should be read by the whole world!"

—Ms. S.S., Lynnwood, Washington

"The stories break my heart, but it is comforting to know there
is hope for them. I feel God has called me to be part of that
hope so people can come to know Jesus Christ."

—Ms. M.R., Knoxville, Tennessee

No Longer a Slumdog

K.P. YOHANNAN

NO LONGER A SLUMDOG

BRINGING HOPE TO CHILDREN IN NEED

BOOKS

A DIVISION OF GOSPEL FOR ASIA
WWW.GFA.ORG

All Scripture quotations, unless otherwise indicated, are taken from the HOLY BIBLE, NEW INTERNATIONAL VERSION ®. Copyright © 1973, 1978, 1984 Biblica. Used by permission of Zondervan. All rights reserved.

Scripture quotations marked KJV are taken from the King James Version. Public Domain.

Scripture quotations marked NASB are taken from the NEW AMERICAN STANDARD BIBLE®, Copyright © 1960, 1962, 1963, 1968, 1971, 1972, 1973, 1975, 1977, 1995 by The Lockman Foundation. Used by permission.

Scripture quotations marked NKJV are taken from the New King James Version. Copyright © 1982 by Thomas Nelson, Inc. Used by permission. All rights reserved.

Scripture quotations marked ESV are from the ESV® Bible (The Holy Bible, English Standard Version®), copyright © 2001 by Crossway, a publishing ministry of Good News Publishers. Used by permission. All rights reserved.

Paperback ISBN: 978-1-59589-172-3

Library of Congress Control Number: 2017932574

Published by gfa books, a division of Gospel for Asia
1116 St. Thomas Way, Wills Point, TX 75169 USA
Phone: (800) 946-2742

Printed in the United States of America

For information about other materials, visit our website: www.gfa.org.

First printing, June 2011   Seventh printing, April 2014
Second printing, July 2011   Eighth printing, August 2014
Third printing, August 2011   Ninth printing, February 2015
Fourth printing, March 2012   Tenth printing, September 2015
Fifth printing, June 2012   Eleventh printing, April 2017
Sixth printing, November 2013

*W*ith love, I dedicate this book

to the thousands of children

who have found new life and a bright future

through GFA's Bridge of Hope Program.

It brings me so much joy

to see you grow in grace and love.

May your light shine brightly

in the world around you.

TABLE OF CONTENTS

FOREWORD

Before I comment on this book, let me first say a few words about my friend K.P. Yohannan. There are few (maybe no) men I respect more than him. In our day and age, it is hard to find a man who can lead thousands while diverting attention away from himself and onto Jesus. God has graced K.P. Yohannan with this type of humility while he leads millions.

I was able to spend several days with K.P. in India in 2010. It was an honor to spend extended time with one of my heroes. I learned a lot from his wisdom and was surprised by his humor (for some reason, I didn't expect him to be that funny). He is simple—you would never know he is the leader of a massive ministry. His most impressive trait, however, is his love. I left our time absolutely shocked by how loved I felt. You would think that love would flow from all Christian leaders, but sadly, it is a rare trait. I thank God for his friendship and support. The reason why I am endorsing this book and asking you to join in its vision and passion is based on him, the leader of this movement, who follows the Lord and hears His voice.

India is the saddest place I have ever visited. Poverty—coupled with spiritual darkness—makes it one of the most miserable places on earth. These people are stuck in an awful cycle. Smiles are rare, and there is an empty sadness in their eyes. While I have not met the individuals mentioned in this book, I can attest there are many who live under similar conditions.

It is in these conditions that I also have witnessed the transforming work of the Gospel. God is using GFA as a light in that world and to millions in more than a dozen nations in Asia, such as Nepal, Myanmar, Bangladesh and so on.

As you read this book, I would encourage you to remember that these are real people we are talking about. They are human beings created in the image of God by a holy God—some of whom you will be hanging out with for all eternity!

In my early days, I would see images on the television of suffering people overseas. I would quickly switch the channel because I did not want to see the suffering. I certainly did not take the time to think of them as individuals with names, lives, families and souls that are just as valuable as my own. I merely labeled them as the "needy" rather than lovely people with personalities. Work hard at seeing their worth. Pray and work for them, as you would want them to do for you if the tables were turned.

I am very thankful for the book you are about to read. It has stirred my heart once again. Living in the West with all of its affluence, it is easy to forget about others. I get focused on my own problems. I forget that one of the best ways to get my mind off myself is by praying for and serving those with greater needs. It is a wonderful opportunity the Lord has given us. We GET to represent Him on this earth by rescuing others as He has rescued us. Few blessings in life compare to the joy we experience when we are used by God to bless those in need.

One of the phrases Jesus used often was "he who has ears, let him hear." His point was that some people change whenever they hear the simple truth. They have "ears to hear." Others will not be affected no matter how clever a message they hear. My guess is that you are reading this book because God has already changed your heart and given you a great love for those in need. Many of us just need to be reminded. Thank you, K.P., for reminding us once again of the amazing privilege we have to represent Christ by serving the poor.

Pastor Francis Chan
Author of *Crazy Love*

ACKNOWLEDGMENTS

Many people have left their mark upon this text and on my heart as they shared their stories with me. I think of Doug Nichols, who pinned me down years ago to be an advocate for the suffering children in this world. I never knew what saying yes would mean. And I am sure this book is in part the fruit of his prayers.

To all the staff who work in GFA-supported Bridge of Hope centers, I thank you. Without your work and your prayers, these children would never have blossomed, and we never would know what the Lord's hand had done.

Thank you to everyone who has enabled a child to step out of darkness and poverty into the light of Christ. Without your support, these children would still be suffering.

Thank you to my staff who have stood with me during the writing of this book. You have given your lives in labor and intercession reaching all across Asia.

Thank you, John—without your impetus, this may never have gotten started.

Kim, thank you for gathering everything together in the beginning and wrapping it all up in the end.

Megan, thank you for your labor of love in working nonstop for months to transcribe, compile and edit this book.

Teresa, my executive secretary, thank you for your unwavering commitment to oversee this project, making sure it was done with the passion I have for these children in crisis.

Thank you, David, for your excellent job in helping to edit this book.

Thank you, Cindy, for the wonderful cover. It has grown on me ever since I saw it.

Special thanks are due to my wife, Gisela, without whose encouragement I would have stumbled many times more than I already have. Your constant companionship and faithfulness have blessed me more than you will ever know.

Most of all, I remain grateful to the Lord Jesus Christ for His constant mercy and grace.

Terms and Concepts

Aryan

The Aryan race, a group of people with fair skin, invaded the Indian subcontinent from Eurasia more than 3,000 years ago. The name *Aryan* means "royal" or "noble." Because these people believed themselves to be better than the indigenous peoples, the caste system was devised to prevent them from becoming "contaminated" by the darker-skinned natives. Aryans, of course, established themselves as the highest caste.

Caste/Caste System

A caste system divides people into groups or "castes" based on their heredity, granting status and privilege to some groups while denying it to others. This insidious system segregates the population and turns people against each other based purely on their genetics.

Dalit/Untouchable

The word *Dalit* literally means "broken," "crushed" or "oppressed." In South Asian society, Dalits are at the lowest rung of the ladder. The vast majority of them are impoverished, exploited and powerless to change their fate. Considered to be polluted or unclean, they are called "Untouchables." If they were to touch someone of higher caste, the upper-caste person would supposedly become contaminated. This is why many Dalits are not allowed to drink from community wells and are discouraged from attending schools with other students.

Other Backward Castes (OBCs)

The term *OBC* applies to those from the lowest castes, also known as *Sudras*. The OBCs are higher than Dalits but are still oppressed and impoverished. *Sudras* are thought of as the slave caste.

Slum

With great numbers of people moving to cities in hope of a better life, the population inevitably grows faster than what the government can sustain. The result is millions of people living in destitute conditions. "Slum" is the name given to the areas where such poor people dwell. These people have no homes, no land, no plumbing or infrastructure and often no education. Most slums are filled with Dalits and OBCs.

Introduction

Have you seen the award-winning movie *Slumdog Million-aire?*[1] If you haven't yet, you should. I can't think of anything that has made me sad like certain scenes in this movie have.

In the film, you see the harvesting of street children by a deceitful, greedy pimp. His bottom line is to get them to beg and collect money for him. He even turns some into sex slaves!

One of the most gruesome parts of the movie is when a 7- or 8-year-old boy is blinded by this cruel man. The pimp actually poured boiling oil into the boy's eyes. A few years later he is seen, still begging, standing in a dark tunnel off a busy street in Bombay. For those caught in begging rings, there is always this fear of being mutilated by a boss in order to gain more sympathy with passersby. Kids who have been disfigured can bring in more money for their pimp. Although this treatment is the exception, there are nonetheless millions of children trapped in a life of begging. I wish these scenes were only fiction in a movie, but unfortunately, what is depicted is reality for countless youngsters.

Each beggar child has some sad story as to how he or she ended up on the streets of Delhi or Dhaka . . . and there they are exploited by those who find them.

In South Asia, there are more than 50 million children who work from age 4 on.[2] They labor from morning until night for pennies, often making only 10–15 cents per day. The majority are Dalits or from one of the Other Backward Castes (OBCs).

These children live in enormous crisis, and I assure you that their suffering causes great pain in the heart of the Living God. At the same time, they present us with a tremendous opportunity to bring hope into their worlds through God's love. They are a part of the 4/14 Window, the 1.2 billion children on this planet between the ages of 4 and 14.[3] As followers of Christ, we are told by our Lord not to neglect, not to ignore, not to forget these precious, helpless children.

GFA helps to support missionaries and social workers who serve among the 1 million dwellers in the Dharavi slum in Bombay[4] where the movie *Slumdog Millionaire* was shot. GFA's Bridge of Hope Program is reaching out to needy children like these all across Asia. In Christ's name we are currently helping to rescue 75,000 children from a life of bondage (as of 2015). Each one is enrolled in a Bridge of Hope center. But what is that compared to the millions of children trapped in a life of hopeless wandering on the streets?

My heart's cry is, "Lord, enable us to rescue at least 500,000 children from despair and hopelessness. Please help us be a part of rescuing these boys and girls from a future of being blinded, maimed, disfigured or forced into the life of a street beggar."

I am sure your heart, like mine, can feel the pain of these precious children. Together we can make a difference, and we will. We must.

Thank you for joining me on this journey to learn more about these precious little ones who are desperately crying out for hope.

Sometime in your life, hope that you might see one

starved man, the look on his face when the bread finally

arrives. Hope that you might have baked it or bought

or even kneaded it yourself. For that look on his face,

for your meeting his eyes across a piece of bread, you

might be willing to lose a lot, or suffer a lot,

or die a little, even.

Daniel Berrigan[1]

CHAPTER ONE

Stolen Childhood

Muttu was born in a small hut in a South Asian slum. His parents died when he was barely 7 years old. His uncle took Muttu and his younger sister to live with him. Unfortunately, this man was an alcoholic and a drug addict and would often both starve and abuse Muttu and his sister.

One day the two children were taken to a neighboring state and sold to Rajan, a beggar mafia pimp. Here they became part of a group of beggar children involving at least 10 others about their age. They were told to beg on the streets and return all the money they collected to Rajan. Muttu became afraid when the other children warned him that he would be severely beaten if he didn't bring back enough money.

Every night Rajan came, often drunk, and took what money the kids had collected that day. On one occasion Muttu did not earn enough to please Rajan. Rajan became irate and beat the helpless lad. In the end, Muttu was dragged to a distant place where Rajan continued to punish him. As Muttu cried out, the angry pimp forcefully closed the young boy's mouth. Then Rajan took a can of kerosene and poured it over Muttu. He set the child's body on fire and left him to die.

Fortunately, someone found him, lying unconscious and covered with rags, and took him to the hospital. More than 50 percent of his body was covered with burns. Even after Muttu regained consciousness, he was unable to say a word for several weeks. For months he suffered excruciating pain.

Muttu did eventually recover, but he still lives in a state of fear. He says the worst part of the whole experience is the agony of not knowing what happened to his little sister.

This story first appeared in a newspaper under the title "A Lonely Battle for Life."

We cannot even begin to imagine something like this being thrust onto a child. It is harsh, it is cruel, and it never should happen. But the sad reality is that it did occur.

When I hear stories like this, I think back on my own life growing up, reflecting on the many blessings and hardships that I faced. It helps me see things from a different perspective.

Let me ask you, what was your childhood like? Your parents probably started planning for you even before your conception. Your medical care began while you were still in your mother's womb. In all likelihood, your mother gave birth to you in a sterile hospital room, surrounded by well-trained doctors and nurses.

After a clean and safe delivery, you probably were taken home to a wallpapered nursery and brand-new baby blankets. You were fed on demand and kept warm, clean and protected from harm. To prevent any serious illnesses, you received all the required immunizations. As you grew into a healthy child, you were given clean clothes to wear and toys to play with.

When you reached school age, your parents took you to the store to buy your school supplies. If you were like most children, your mom sent you off to school in bright new clothes with a nourishing lunch. Maybe she even drove you there herself.

Does this treatment of children sound strange or unusual? Not at all. It is completely normal in countries and homes of financial means. Even acknowledging that there are unfortunate exceptions, I doubt anyone reading this book would disagree that this kind of security, provision and education are a child's birthright.

A Far Different Reality

The reality for children born in developing countries is often a far cry from what I just described. The tragedy for untold millions of children living today is that they have never had even *one* of these childhood experiences. Imagine if this was you:

Your parents saw your conception as both a blessing and a curse. They knew that in a few years there would be more hands to work, but also that you would put even more strain on the meager food supply. Prenatal care for you was lacking because there were no medical facilities in the remote village or slum where you were born and your parents could not afford to travel away from home to find one.

After a risky home delivery on the dirt floor of the family shack, you were dried off with a dirty rag or an old newspaper; your parents never learned much about sanitation.

Your home was made of tarpaulin sheets held up by bamboo sticks. It was pretty crowded with your whole family living in less than 100 square feet of space. The shack was right next to a railroad track, and every 10 minutes a train would come roaring through. Sleep was difficult under these conditions.

When you were born, you were already malnourished. The little milk your mother was able to give you couldn't do much to

Many children throughout the world live in a perpetual state of hunger and pain, their bodies struggling to keep up with the demands that are placed on them.

ensure your growth. You might also suffer night-blindness from vitamin A deficiency.

Soon your mom had to resume her day job of cleaning streets with a hand-broom and washing other people's clothes, because when she didn't work, the family didn't eat. So you were left in the care of an older sibling. As you started to crawl, you explored on your hands and knees the open sewer trenches running along the alley between neighboring shacks. If you had any clothing at all, it was made from rags found in the nearby dump, which is where all the household treasures came from.

If through strength and providence you survived the first few years of life, at the age of 5 or 6 you might be sold by your parents into bonded labor to help secure a little desperately needed money for the family. Otherwise, you probably joined your siblings sifting through garbage to find rags, plastic bottles, pieces of metal or anything else that could be sold for a few pennies to help the family survive. You may have become a beggar or even a thief, desperately doing whatever you could just to eat.

School? It wasn't even a possibility. Your small contribution to the family income was needed just to survive. Besides, nobody in the family had ever been to school anyway.

You think I'm exaggerating. No, I am not. According to UNICEF, more than *1 billion children* around the world are deprived of one or more of these essentials: adequate shelter, food, safe water, sanitation, health care or education—living in conditions you and I can hardly imagine.[2]

DESPERATE POVERTY

As bad as this sounds, millions of children every year experience a far worse fate. In despair of ever being able to care for you, your mother might one day have thrust you onto a passing train bound for an Asian metropolis. At the end of the run, you would have been pushed onto the streets of a megacity by a train employee as you screamed in vain for your mommy. It is hard to imagine this could really happen—but it does. I heard this very story told by a girl named Asha. Here's her tale in her own words:

My name is Asha. Six months ago, my sister Lata and I got on a train with our mom. She told us we were going to Bombay. We were excited because all the movies in India are made in Bombay! We love watching movies, and we always wanted to ride a train.

Lata and I pushed through the other passengers and squeezed into our seats with our mother. We had a lot of fun looking out the windows at all the trees and fields passing by. The train made stop after stop at junctions along the way. I did not know when we would get there, but I thought it must be soon because we had traveled so far. At one of the stops, Mom stood up and said to us, "You girls stay here. I'm going to get something to drink." But after a few minutes, the train started moving again, and Mom still wasn't back!

We were so scared that we didn't know what to do! We held our hands together and stayed as close as we could. Our hearts were racing. The train left the junction and kept going faster and faster. Hours passed. Where was Mom? No one seemed to know or care.

After many hours, the train finally stopped at a big, loud station. I was in tears. I decided that we should get off. There were people everywhere, pushing and shoving. Lata and I stayed close together, but we did not know where to go. I thought that maybe someone could help us, but I was too scared to talk to anyone! We sat together in a corner, waiting for something to happen. I don't know what. We waited for several hours.

As the sun started to set, a kind-looking woman came and asked us what was wrong. We told her that we had lost our mother. She led us to a shelter where we could stay, a place for other girls who were lost or didn't have their families.

It feels like it has been a long time since that day. Our mother still has not found us, but I am glad we are at the shelter. I don't know what would have happened to us if we had stayed at the station.

Due to acute poverty in the rural villages, abandoning children is a choice that some parents are almost forced to make. An online search reveals even more about the horrible situations in which children in this generation find themselves trapped.

In India alone, there are 11 million children like Asha who have been abandoned, and 90 percent of them are girls.[3] Three million of these children end up living on the streets.[4]

We encountered one such street child just outside a GFA-supported Bridge of Hope center; she had been living on the railroad tracks. At about three in the afternoon, as all the students were going home, one of the staff members saw a little girl standing all alone with her head down, weeping and not saying a word. She couldn't have been more than 9 years old.

The teacher approached her to ask what was wrong, but she could not stop crying. Eventually, in barely a whisper, these words came out: "My brother also died."

Then her story started to tumble out. Her parents had died several years earlier, and she had been left living on the railroad tracks with her brother. That was until he, too, recently passed away.

The little girl said that the children she used to play with were all gone. They left her and were now in the center. So she had come to ask, "Would you take me too?"

Due to the acute poverty throughout southern Asia, almost half of the children there live without adequate shelter. Some have homes made of whatever materials they can find, while others simply sleep on the streets.

Of course we did. But the sad reality remains that most such children do not find a place of hope like this.

Throughout the slums of Asia, there are millions of children living with only one of their parents. Many dads and moms have died because of easily preventable diseases. Some are simply overworked, their bodies failing because of exhaustion and undernourishment. If the father is gone, it becomes even harder for a family to survive. There is a huge social stigma attached to being a widow that makes it very difficult for the mom to get a job.

Even when both parents are alive, they spend so much time working menial jobs just to survive, like cleaning streets or working in a landlord's field, that they end up with few hours to spend at home with their kids. Children left in such conditions easily become rowdy and uncontrollable.

This is just what happened to two young boys. Their father had left the family in order to go to a big city, where he thought he could make some money. Vichy and Tusli, ages 9 and 7, quickly became quite disobedient.

The father had thoughtfully left their mother some money to help care for the family while he was gone. Vichy and Tusli promptly stole it and wasted it.

Their lives were spinning out of control. They would wander around the slum stealing from people, harassing other children and generally being troublemakers. Everyone considered these boys a headache, but no one knew what to do with them. Many were actually afraid of them and didn't want to stir up any trouble for themselves.

When Yadav, the leader of the local Bridge of Hope center, found out about the plight of this family, he was burdened by the Lord to help. He made arrangements for these two brothers to be enrolled in the center. It took a great deal of patience just to get these unruly boys to sit through their lessons. Yadav devoted a lot of his time to helping them and would pray for them as he taught them how to live. Slowly he instilled discipline into them and demonstrated respect and kindness while sharing lessons from the Bible.

Without an education, impoverished children have almost no chance of ever escaping the hardship in which they are trapped.

The two boys started to change, and eventually, their lives turned around completely. Now Vichy, the older one, likes to visit the same people he used to harass and share the love of Christ with them. Instead of calling him "headache," now the people in the slum are glad when he shows up.

God is able to work amazing transformations in the lives of such children, and we have seen Him using Bridge of Hope to bring hope into their lives. But for the millions of children still waiting in the rural villages and slums, there remains little chance of change unless someone can step in and help.

Calcutta alone is home to more than 100,000 street children[5] who know neither father nor mother, love nor care. They are left to fend for themselves, resorting to whatever means necessary just to survive.

One of the most shocking reports I ever read appeared in the

Indian Express several years ago. On the front page was a photo of a little boy, half naked, lying on the sidewalk of a busy street. Next to the boy was a dog. Upon closer inspection, I saw that it was a female dog, and the little boy was actually sucking her milk. The caption read, "This Dog Is His Mother." The three-column article went on to describe the heartbreaking agony that homeless children face as they try to survive on their own.

That article came out several years ago, and I wish I could report that things have gotten better. But I can't because the media keep telling me otherwise.

During one of our weekly prayer meetings, a staff member presented a story he had read recently on the BBC News website.[6] Here was a photo of two little children, maybe 3 or 4 years old. Their stomachs were distended eight to ten inches out from their bodies. They lived near a quarry where their parents worked. The earnings from their backbreaking hours of labor produced enough for only one meal a day. In their desperate hunger, the children had eaten mud from the quarry, making them sick. In fact, one of the two was already showing signs of early kidney failure.

It breaks my heart to see such suffering, especially knowing this has been going on much longer than I have been alive.

CRUEL EXPLOITATION

Children in underdeveloped countries are often the victims of cruel exploitation of various kinds. Throughout the world, more than 150 million children between the ages of 4 and 14 are involved in child labor.[7] There are 1.2 million children bought and sold every year.[8] Those who end up on the streets are quickly picked up, like the boys in the movie *Slumdog Millionaire,* and forced into a begging ring or other hard labor. Child laborers of Asia toil to make fireworks, twist carpet fibers or make matches in primitive factories. They spend their days in quarries and coal mines, rice fields, tea plantations and pastures.

One girl labored in the fields of a cottonseed farm in southern India, earning 20 cents an hour. This 15-year-old was continually exposed to the highly toxic pesticides that were sprayed on the fields every week, where she has been working since she was 10. She started working when her father committed suicide after incurring huge debts.[9]

An article in *Forbes* magazine tells of six to eight young boys crammed together in a room no bigger than a king-size bed. They work 16 hours a day, decorating photo frames, diaries, shoe heels and such with sequins and pieces of glass. Some are as young as 5 years old. They all live together in this same room and cook their food together. Their combined earnings each month might be US$76,[10] which means each child only makes US$9.50 each month!

The worst fate of all awaits little girls who end up trapped in prostitution. Some are kidnapped or tricked into it. Parents sometimes sell their girls, similar to the way children are sold into bonded labor. Others are dedicated to this life as a sort of offering by their parents. The book *Dalit Freedom* brings this practice to light.

> Thousands of untouchable female children (between six and eight years old) are forced to become maidens of God. . . . They are taken from

their families, never to see them again. They are later raped by the temple priest and finally auctioned secretly into prostitution and ultimately die.[11]

Other girls, and some boys, are simply caught on the streets or kidnapped from their homes. There are more than 1.2 million children involved in prostitution throughout the Indian subcontinent; many of them are from Nepal or Bangladesh.[12] Children's Care International explains:

> Recruiting children for the purposes of prostitution is done in the same way as for child labourers: they are bought and sold. Many children, however, are simply kidnapped. . . . The little girls find themselves locked up in brothels or end up in national and international prostitution networks. The children must first reimburse the money given to their parents plus the interest—an astronomical amount that becomes an eternal debt. They are forced to remain sexual slaves because of this debt, which is impossible to reimburse because it increases daily. . . . The majority of these children suffer from serious physical and psychological problems, and their life expectancy is about 15 years.[13]

My heart aches as I hear what is happening to God's innocent creations. It is hard to realize this is not a novel, this is not a movie, and this is not even a nightmare. This is reality—reality for millions of children on the earth at this very hour.

The reason for such brutality, pain, abuse and all suffering is, in a word, sin. This sort of agony is not the way God meant

Millions of children are trapped in bonded labor, sold into prostitution or abandoned every year.

for us to live when He created us. But Satan came to destroy, tear down and kill (see John 10:10), and he is at the source of this heartache, leaving these children hurting and destitute.

Looking into their faces, you won't see innocence and trust, but rather hunger, pain, suspicion and fear.

When we see their plight, we ask ourselves, why is this happening? Is there an answer to their suffering? Who are these desperate children in crisis, and what can we do to bring them hope?

 "You hear, O LORD, the desire of the afflicted; you encourage them, and you listen to their cry, defending the fatherless and the oppressed, in order that man, who is of the earth, may terrify no more" (Psalm 10:17–18).

*T*he *biggest disease today is not leprosy or tuberculosis,*

but rather the feeling of being unwanted.

Mother Teresa[1]

CHAPTER TWO

ONCE A SLUMDOG, ALWAYS A SLUMDOG

A few years ago, a story appeared in a major newspaper that revealed once again the plight of the desperate, suffering people of Asia. The story was shocking; a young and destitute mother sold her newborn for 10 pounds of rice!

I could hardly believe what I was reading. A picture was included of this fragile yet truly beautiful girl, maybe in her mid-20s, with tears running down her face. She was crying as she told the reporter, "I want my baby back."

When she was asked, "Why would you sell your baby for 10 pounds of rice?" her answer was even more disturbing. She replied, "What do we do? People like us are starving to death . . . at least my baby will live. I will die anyway, like many others here. Even the 10 pounds of rice will not save me."

Poverty, grief and hopelessness were etched on her face and the faces of those who flocked around her.

WHO ARE THESE PEOPLE?

These are the Dalits and the Other Backward Castes.

They have had to break their malnourished bodies, working

all hours of the day simply to get enough money for one meal. Why? It is more than just poverty, though they are among the poorest in the world. It is more than just their lack of education, though only 30 percent of them can read at all.[2] It is because of the caste system and the fact that they are not a part of it.

This oppressive way of life for the world's most impoverished all began with the arrival of the Aryans to the Indian subcontinent about 1500 B.C. Because the Aryans believed themselves to be a superior race, they devised a cruel system to prevent themselves from becoming "contaminated" by the indigenous peoples. This system also served to help control the populace, making them view each other through a distorted lens of inequality.

Through this tactic, the Aryans were quickly able to become a rich and highly educated minority. Instead of using physical weapons, they used this mind-bending tool called the caste system. This system taught that people were reborn from different parts of the body of their deity and thus had differing value.

Thousands of years later, people still believe that those who came from the head, arms and shoulders are intrinsically better than those who came from the torso, legs or feet. This is the premise and justification used to abuse those of lower caste.

The caste system also divided society based on roles or jobs. The four main castes, from the greatest to the least, are *Brahmins* (priests and teachers), *Kshatriyas* (rulers and soldiers), *Vaisyas* (merchants and traders) and *Sudras* (laborers and servants). Within these four main castes, there are countless subcastes that further divide and categorize the population.

Caste is determined at birth. If, for example, your parents were of high caste, you would also be of that caste. However, if your parents were low caste, that's where you would belong. You would grow up learning to fear and respect those who are higher and despise those who are lower.

There is no opportunity for advancement, no hope of some-day being worth more. Whatever you are, you always will be.

Your caste not only affects your sense of worth, but also the jobs you can hold, what clothes you can wear, where you can wor-ship, who you can marry, where you can gather water and what sort of education you can expect.

The caste system, though officially outlawed in India, is still a major source of social identity and ostracism. It is because of their caste that many of these children suffer.

This pervasive system of social ostracism and prejudice is the glue that keeps everyone in their proper place, even where caste-based discrimination is officially prohibited by law.

THE BOTTOM OF THE BOTTOM

At the very bottom of the system, below all four castes and all the subcastes, is a group of people called "Untouchables" or "Dalits." The word *Dalit* means "oppressed" or "broken." They are considered by other castes to be subhuman, impure from birth and worthy of nothing but contempt. To be "Untouchable" means just that—no upper-caste can touch you, and you cannot touch them either. Anything you contact is declared unclean. If anyone were to stoop low enough to give you something to eat or drink, be assured that it will be in a cheap disposable dish. Further, it is expected that *you* will throw away what you just "contaminated."

Often Dalits are denied access to public wells for the same fear of contamination. In an article published October 25, 2010, I read of three Dalit men who received heavy fines because they drank from a public water fountain used by the upper-castes.[3]

The majority of these exploited peoples live in rural villages and communities, slaving away to eke out a living. But there are also millions of Dalits and OBCs who try to live crammed into the slums. Those on the outside looking into the slums began to see these people in the same way they saw the wild animals that run down the narrow dirt streets. This is where the name "slumdog" comes from.

I cannot fully imagine what it would be like to be a Dalit, even though I have seen and read so much. The following poem helps shed light on what it must be like. It is written from the perspective of one of their children.

> I am nobody
> Worthless my life is
> To Untouchables I was born.
> A Dalit child my fate sealed.
>
> I was born in slums
> Rights? We have none
> To upper-caste our lives we owe
> Slaves to serve all their wish.
>
> Poverty and hunger
> Is all I ever knew
> If there is hope
> Tell me how?
>
> What is my future?
> Do I have any?
> It all looks so dark
> And I wish I was not born.[4]

For 3,000 years, hundreds of millions of Untouchables have suffered slavery and oppression at the hands of their fellow countrymen. Many truly believe they have earned this life and have no right to expect anything different.

Heart-Wrenching Decisions

Often the Dalits are driven to extreme measures just to make ends meet. I don't know how they can stand making these heart-wrenching decisions, such as giving away an 8-year-old son or daughter to be a bonded laborer for an upper-caste landlord or selling their body as a prostitute. Then they must live with the mental anguish of making such choices.

I recently heard of a young woman who had to make such a decision. In the year 2000, Geeta was married at the young age of 17. She had her first daughter just a year later in 2001. Shortly after their marriage, her husband lost his job, got involved in illegal activities and became an alcoholic. In early 2003, he left Geeta while she was pregnant with their second child, a son.

Totally alone, Geeta started going from house to house, washing dishes to make a little money. She would also make floral garlands to sell, but it was never enough. There was no one to help her, and she faced her difficult life alone.

Because they lived in the slums, she felt that her children's character was being ruined and their future looked dim. They were often starving or half-fed. Rent was difficult to pay, and education for her children was all but impossible. Geeta hoped her situation would improve, but it only got worse. She eventually became so desperate that she seriously considered selling her half-starved body into prostitution.

It was at this critical juncture in 2006 that a GFA-supported Bridge of Hope center was started in the slum where Geeta lives. Both her children were enrolled, and they were finally getting not only an education and food to eat, but also a stable and safe place to grow. They began to blossom under the teachings of Christ.

Geeta was counseled by the Bridge of Hope staff workers, and they often prayed with her. God in His mercy gave her a laborer's job in a factory. And now that her children are sheltered by the Bridge of Hope center, they have a bright future too.

I praise God that He rescued Geeta from the agony of having to make such a terrible decision. There are still many, however, who have few options for employment. They will do whatever they can just to make enough to eat.

INTENSE LABOR

The filthiest, most degrading and menial work in society is relegated to Dalits. They are the ones who harvest the fields by hand, working for hours in backbreaking labor. They are the ones who clean the open-air toilets, latrines and sewer lines with their bare hands.

I remember hearing the sorrow of a little boy in a GFA-supported Bridge of Hope center who lost his mother. She performed backbreaking labor, toiling all day long. She would go into the nearby forest to collect dead wood. Then she would carry it on her head to the nearby market to sell as firewood. All of this was just to earn a few rupees, an amount that was never quite enough to feed their aching, empty stomachs. I remember feeling his hurt and wrote this poem at the time:

> Dark, skinny body—this was my mother
> Eyes sunken with pain
> Turns and looks at us
> As she disappears into the woods.

It is late in the afternoon
We children had eaten nothing all day
Waiting and watching for mother
After selling the sticks to come home with food.

Our father left for a neighboring state
Looking for a coolie's job
For Untouchables here like us
There is no job except cleaning latrines.

Poverty and hunger took its toll
My mother died without help
My brothers and I did not know what to do
Wandering on streets all day long.

Our father came home a broken man
Held us in his arms crying bitterly
He sits and gazes into the dark
Mutters to himself I don't know what.

The sun rose with bright hope
Some kind people took us to school
At first I didn't know much at all
Now I know we have hope.

Often my eyes seek my mother
I still cry and grieve
When I see a dark skinny vendor of wood,
I wish I had money to buy her sticks.[5]

And we all wish there was some way we could help.

I am so glad that this boy was able to find hope in the midst
of his grief. But the sad truth is that all too many have yet to hear

of this God of hope and are breaking under the burden they carry, thinking that only a life of hurt awaits them.

Excluded from the caste system, "Untouchables" do all the tasks that others consider "unclean," including disposing of corpses, cleaning up human waste and performing other labor-intensive jobs. Like the woman in the poem, people can often be seen carrying large loads that strain their fragile bodies.

DEVOID OF RIGHTS

Those at the bottom are routinely denied even the most basic human rights. Violence is rampant. Degradation against Dalits is so pervasive that one country passed something called the "Prevention of Atrocities Act," spelling out the illegality of such things as parading people naked through the streets, forcing them to eat feces or burning down their houses. Nevertheless, thousands of acts of public humiliation and group violence, such as lynching and gang rape, continue to take place. It seems that the rules of untouchability don't apply to acts of violence or sexual abuse against Dalits.

A Dalit might be beaten to death just for asking for his daily wages. On June 16, 2009, an article in a newspaper reported that a 48-year-old Dalit laborer had been attacked by a group of men after asking he be paid his salary that had already been withheld for an entire month. Five men in total attacked and killed the Dalit worker by beating him mercilessly with wooden sticks.[6]

For the most part, Dalits have no one to turn to for help. Because they are at the bottom rung of the proverbial social ladder, they have little chance of ever getting their case through the courts.

Crimes against Dalits are rarely reported to authorities because of the fear of reprisal. Sadly, the police will often turn a blind eye even when they know the full story.

I remember hearing of a Dalit girl who was raped by several men. Her parents were told by the girl's attackers not to go to the police, but they did anyway. A few days later, they found the dead body of their daughter lying in a field.

It is nearly impossible for us to imagine the mental anguish Dalits live with, growing up as children in a society that views them as expendable, being called worthless and treated with contempt. We must hurry to reach those who continue to live in pain and darkness. Worse than all the abuse, than all the discrimination, the backbreaking labor and constant hunger are the feelings of hopelessness they experience every day.

STUCK IN THE CYCLE

All too many Dalits get trapped in bonded labor, a kind of indentured servant arrangement in which poor families can pay what they owe through work. In hopes of clearing debts faster, it is not only the parents who are involved, but their children as well. Often the whole family will work for the lender, usually someone who is in an upper caste.

Some families were sold into servitude when the parents were still children and never escaped it. The debt to a landowner or employer may be small, but the interest rate charged often exceeds what they are paid. The result then is that they can never repay what they owe. This is especially true when these poor people are illiterate, as they often are. Because they cannot read or write, they are incapable of keeping records of the work they have done, the amount they owe or the amount they have repaid.

But beyond being trapped in debt and bonded labor, their mindset is also ensnared.

The conditioning works something like this: you can tie a dog to a stake, and it will run in a circle. After a long time, you can actually remove the stake and the dog will still run in the same circle. It no longer thinks of going into the field because it is so accustomed to the limitations of the rope. It accepts that it cannot go any further, so it stops trying.

Likewise, Dalits have lived their entire lives thinking there is nothing better for them, that there is no hope of change or

Millions are trapped by their caste, stuck in the mindset that things cannot change and will not change.

freedom. For them, it does feel that their fate truly is "once a slumdog, always a slumdog."

Niran John Das grew up living in this as reality, until one day everything changed.

> *I was born and brought up in a Dalit society where we were very much oppressed and downtrodden by the higher people. There are a lot of people who practice untouchability here, who won't share a bench with someone from a low caste or share food with them or anything.*
>
> *I went to school up to third grade, but I had to discontinue when my father became ill. Suddenly*

there was no one to support the family, so I, being the eldest son, had to start working. My dreams were all shattered. I worked in house construction, making and carrying bricks or cultivating the barley and wheat fields.

We didn't have breakfast, and we didn't have lunch; all that we had was dinner. I was so hurt and very sad when I saw that we worked hard the whole day but only made enough for one meal while others who didn't work as hard had more than enough. We were sometimes paid late, and then there was no food at home.

Sometimes we would take a debt to pay for our rent, and then we would have to take more. You know, it is kind of a cycle. You get debt and you work. You are not able to pay back and so you keep working for them. And that's what used to happen to us.

Even when my father became well enough to work, we still could not afford school for any of us. Our family and our needs had grown. He went to the neighboring state to look for a job and took me with him.

While we were there, he came to know the Lord Jesus and became the first believer in our village. My father used to pray and read the Bible and take me to church. But I was not interested at that time and went back to my home village.

Later I was married, and we both were working for the landlords. I always wondered, When are we going to improve this situation? I have to get liberated from all this kind of bondage.

And it is a bondage. But the problem was, even

though I wanted to get freedom from this, I could not because we were not educated. I didn't understand how to get liberated. I wanted freedom, but there was no way to get out. In the society that I grew up in, it is destined. I could not become a higher-caste person because the cycle is always there, and this is what I believed. It was all normal life for us.

After some years, I became sick and could not tell east from west, and I could hardly stand. My family did all sorts of religious rituals for my healing, but nothing worked. My father came, and for six years he prayed for my healing, shared about Jesus and encouraged me. But then one night, he asked some other Christians he knew to pray for my healing. My family who did not know the Lord said, "If Jesus can heal him, then we will accept Jesus as our Savior." That was the challenge they set.

As my father prayed, I felt a strange kind of feeling. The next morning, I was able to ride my bike again. I was completely healed. The whole village was shocked. They had not known Christ could do such a thing.

Because of this miracle, I gave my life to the Lord. I understood that I was freed from the bondages of the caste system. In Christ, there is no high caste and no low caste. And when the barrier is not there, I'm no longer under bondage. I'm free only in Christ.

And this is what I love. My main desire is to go and make people here in the village realize that we can be freed. If people can realize there is no difference in a person, whether from a Dalit society or from high society, their bondage will be broken. Their eyes will be opened. So I always pray, every day, that the people in my village should realize we are all the same in Christ.

I praise God that the cycle of oppressive thinking Niran John Das had lived with all his life was finally broken through the all-surpassing love of Christ. This man has been completely transformed. From a life of thinking he was worthless and destined to perpetual servitude, he has now embraced his dignity and freedom in Christ. I pray there will be many more who experience this miracle!

A Scourge in Our Times

Most of the unfortunate children who beg on the streets of South Asia's cities, labor in its fields and factories or die a thousand deaths as child prostitutes are Dalits. They are the most disenfranchised of the disenfranchised, the least of the least, the little ones who have no power to change their world. So they remain as they are, trapped in the slums and the fields of Asia.

In the Subcontinent today, there are about *250 million* Dalits. That means almost 20 percent of the population is considered subhuman and treated like dogs.[7] Seventy percent of Dalits live below the poverty line, and at most 3 percent of Dalit women can read and write.[8]

Slightly above Dalits on the caste ladder is another huge group of people, an estimated 500 million more.[9] They belong to the Other Backward Castes. They also suffer abuse and injustice at the hands of the upper-caste minority. The two groups combined represent a population that is well over twice that of the United States. In fact, more than one out of every 10 people alive on planet earth today is either a Dalit or an OBC.

Can you think of any system in history that has so adversely affected such a large percentage of the world's population as this scourge of the caste system has? I can't.

These masses of people grow up without hearing about the love of Jesus. They live without peace, suspecting there is something fundamentally wrong but not knowing how to change things. These are the "harassed and helpless" Jesus talked about (Matthew 9:36).

One woman among these masses is Indrani. She grew up in a Dalit Gypsy family, traveling from place to place. Her parents taught her how to drink when she was a girl, and also how to smoke, gamble and beg. She thought her ways were normal. Later she lived in a small hut the government granted to her clan. She made maybe US$1 per day through her begging, and her husband made about twice that working on fences. They had eight children, all of them girls.

Indrani did not want her girls to be raised the same way she was but didn't know how she could make a difference in their lives. Thankfully, Indrani met someone who told her about Bridge of Hope. Her girls were soon enrolled.

They learned about Christ, hygiene, discipline and manners, reading, respect and general self-control. But their learning didn't stop with them. The girls took these lessons home.

Indrani marveled at how they were maturing, wishing that

she had such an opportunity when she was young. But then she thought, *If my children are able to change, why can't I?* So she started to pray to the Lord and go to the local fellowship. She gave up her drinking, her gambling and her tobacco use. Now the whole family prays together every day, and they are growing in the Lord.

Although the caste in which they were born dictated that this family would never be able to change, they found a bright future and a new hope in Christ. I hate to think about what the life of Indrani's eight girls would be like if they too grew up believing they were only good enough to be slumdogs and beg for a living.

HOPE AT LAST

God has always been in the business of redemption—just think of the Israelites. He saw their affliction. He heard their cries. He knew their sufferings. And so He came down to deliver them. This is the story we read in the book of Exodus when some 600,000 Israelites were finally freed after 400 years of captivity.

Likewise, God has seen the millions of people who have been living in perpetual servitude for the past 3,000 years. He knows the plight of the child laborers.

We know that God's ears are attentive to the pleas of the captives. Jesus said He came for this very purpose: "The Spirit of the Lord is upon me, because he has anointed me to proclaim good news to the poor. He has sent me to proclaim liberty to the captives and recovering of sight to the blind, to set at liberty those who are oppressed" (Luke 4:18, ESV).

God the Almighty was moved with compassion over the suffering, oppression and slavery of His people, the "children of Israel." It might be interesting to note that the Dalits are also called "Harijan." Although it has now become a derogatory term, it is a name that literally means "children of god." God cares about the suffering of the Dalits as much as He cared about those who were slaves in Egypt.

And how did He respond?

When God saw their suffering, He told Moses, "I have indeed seen the misery of my people in Egypt. I have heard them crying out because of their slave drivers, and I am concerned about their suffering. So I have come down to rescue them from the hand of the Egyptians and to bring them up out of that land into a good and spacious land, a land flowing with milk and honey. . . . I have seen the way the Egyptians are oppressing them. So now, go. *I am sending you*" (Exodus 3:7–10, emphasis mine).

When God spoke to Moses, naturally we might assume that God Himself was coming down to earth to do this rescuing, saving work. Right?

No.

Instead, God says to Moses, "Go. I am sending *you*" (Exodus 3:10, emphasis mine).

If God were coming down to save His people, why did He send Moses? Not because He *needed* Moses' strength and arm of the flesh, but because He chose to work through him, just like God still *works through us* to carry out His will. This is important to recognize. Although God is fully capable of accomplishing all He desires on His own, He still uses us in His incredible work.

God used Moses to guide Israel out of Egypt and to tell the people how to be saved from death through the Passover Lamb. The night after they took shelter under the blood of the lamb, they were led out of their slavery.

Countless millions of Dalit villagers and slum dwellers, including their children, also need to be set free. They have yet to hear of the Lamb that was slain from the foundations of the earth (see Revelation 13:8).

We know the cries of these little children ascend day and night to heaven and that God knows their suffering. There is nothing on earth God is not aware of.

Our hearts ache to change their worlds and make things right. We pray that they too might have life and have it more abundantly. Yet how much more does God Himself yearn for His own creation? He knows all these children personally.

He is the One who said, "It would be better . . . if a millstone were hung around his neck and he were thrown into the sea, than that he would cause one of these little ones to stumble" (Luke 17:2, NASB).

The question is, when *we* hear the cry of the suffering children and the Dalits, can we obey the voice of God and be part of the answer?

I believe we can.

 "I want to lift them up. When I go to villages, even different places, I see people who are without food even. I groan within me. And I think, 'How can I help them come out of all this poverty and oppression and this kind of problem?' That's my burden."

—Niran John Das, missionary

Y*ou can give without loving, but you cannot love*

without giving.

Amy Carmichael[1]

CHAPTER THREE

OPEN YOUR EYES

Long ago there lived a very rich man. He was so wealthy he could buy anything he wanted. His palace, beautifully adorned with all sorts of luxury items, was the largest building for miles. He was able to eat whatever his heart desired. His clothes were stylish and clean, and he had numerous servants. In all his life, he never knew a day of want.

On the street in front of his mansion lived a poor beggar. The only clothes he had were the ones on his back, and they were tattered. His hair was long and scraggly, and he was quite sick. His body was covered with sores, so terrible and oozing that the street dogs came and licked them. Every day he would sit in front of the gates of the rich man's estate, begging for scraps of food. Then one day the poor beggar died, and angels carried him to God's paradise.

In time, the rich man also died. He went directly to hell. He is there to this day, crying out in desperation for just one drop of water to cool his tongue. The response he gets is always the same: "You enjoyed your luxurious life on earth without one thought about the helpless, defenseless beggar who sat by your gates. Now see what has happened. You will suffer in hell and Lazarus, the man you neglected, is in paradise with God. He will live in absolute delight forever, and nothing can take this from him.

Likewise, nothing can change this terrible fate of yours; it is sealed" (see Luke 16:19–25).

Obviously, I have paraphrased the story Jesus told in Luke 16. Please don't misunderstand; the rich man did not go to hell simply because he was rich. If we look through the Bible, there are many people like Abraham, Joseph and David who were all exceedingly rich, even ruling kingdoms and dynasties, and they were completely devoted to God. Their riches did not lead them to their eternal destination. Likewise, it was not poverty that sent Lazarus to heaven.

The reality is, it is not the physical or the obvious externals that become the reason why one goes to heaven, but rather a relationship with God manifested in choices made. The rich man's uncaring attitude toward the poor and suffering revealed his life apart from God. If he knew God in reality and walked with Him, he would have cared for Lazarus. It is plain throughout the Bible that God doesn't want us to ignore the poor, the defenseless, the hungry or the hurting.

Look at Acts 10, where we read the story of a Gentile named Cornelius, a devout man who feared God. Two additional things are written about him. He prayed continually and *gave alms generously to the people.* The inward heart of Cornelius, the devout, God-fearing part, was displayed outwardly in his generosity. God sent His great apostle Peter specifically to meet with this Gentile and share the Good News with him.

God is sad when He sees His people living selfishly, only concerned about "me and mine." It especially hurts Him whenever Christians close their eyes to the pressing needs before them.

Are we like the rich man? My prayer is that we will all take this warning seriously. How many more cars, clothes, toys and trinkets do we really need before we wake up and realize that half the world goes to bed every night with empty stomachs and naked bodies?

Turn through the pages of this book. Look at the faces of these beautiful children God is weeping over. The Lord is looking for those who will share His heart. Open your eyes and look at the reality that is before you.

Remember what Jesus said, "Whatever you did for one of the least of these brothers of mine, *you did for me*" (Matthew 25:40, emphasis mine). This means that whatever we do for the least of these, whether good or bad, it is as though we have done it for Christ Himself. In other words, the beggar Lazarus sitting neglected in front of the rich man's gate was, in reality, God lying there.

When we hear about the millions of suffering, hurting children in the world, let us not look the other way. Each one represents our Lord Himself.

JESUS CARES

Over and over in Scripture, we recognize God's heart for those who have no voice, for the captives and the oppressed. There is a divine passion for them, a heavenly desire for their well-being, because God prizes them highly and His heart breaks to see them suffer.

The Scripture is crystal-clear about God's heart for children. The best place to look is at Jesus, because He is the exact representation of the Father's nature (see Hebrews 1:3). Jesus Himself says, "Anyone who has seen me has seen the Father" (John 14:9).

Therefore, we can be sure the fullness of God's heart for children was perfectly reflected in the life and words of His Son. So what can we learn from Him?

Throughout the Gospels, we see Jesus repeatedly speaking about how important children are to Him and to the Father. In Mark 10, we encounter Jesus surrounded by people, teaching them the truths of God. Some of the parents in the crowd started bringing their children to Him so He could bless them. The disciples rebuked these people and started practicing crowd control. They may have said something like, "The Master is teaching an important message. Please sit down and keep your children quiet."

This passage states that when Jesus saw what was happening, He was displeased and told His disciples, "Let the little children

Jesus would sit and give children His undivided attention, and He commands us to do the same in His name.

Your stamp on this card is like an
additional donation!—Bro. K.P.

fold before tearing

BUSINESS REPLY MAIL
FIRST-CLASS MAIL · PERMIT NO 1 · WILLS POINT TX

POSTAGE WILL BE PAID BY ADDRESSEE

GOSPEL FOR ASIA
1116 ST THOMAS WAY
WILLS POINT TX 75169-9911

**Sponsor a child, get news
from the mission field
and download free
resources at**

GFA.ORG

come to Me, and do not forbid them; for of such is the kingdom of God" (Mark 10:14, NKJV). He actually interrupted His teaching, put His hands on them and blessed them. In the midst of His busy ministry, Jesus stopped everything He was doing to show these children His love and interest.

In Mark 9:37 (NKJV), Jesus said, "Whoever receives one of these little children in My name receives Me." What does His statement mean to us?

Imagine that you have worked all day and are finally sitting down to dinner with your family. Suddenly, you hear a knock on the door. You aren't expecting anyone, so you look through the peephole thinking you will maybe see a salesman or someone who wants to mow your lawn. Instead, you see the King of the universe.

You would break down your front door to welcome Him in!

But what if you see a starving child, half-naked, with more holes than cloth in the rags she is wearing? Her hair is unkempt and filled with lice; her face is covered with dirt and sweat. Would you break down your door to welcome her in?

Jesus tells us that anyone who embraces little children, who loves them and who gives them dignity and value in *His name* is actually doing these same things for Jesus Himself (see Matthew 18:5). But there's more to it than that. Jesus is so happy with anyone who cares for children in His name, that He will come and be with them in a special way. He tells us further in Mark 9:37 that we receive not only the Son, but God the Father also. So there is a special blessing for those who share the heart of the Eternal for His children.

Do Not Despise Them

In Matthew 18:10 (NASB), Jesus said, "See that you do not despise one of these little ones, for I say to you that their angels in heaven continually see the face of My Father who is in heaven." According to the dictionary, the meaning of the word *despise* is "to regard as unworthy of one's interest or concern."

Jesus is warning us that when we hear about needy children, we need to be careful not to see their plight as unworthy of our attention. We can't simply say, "Yes, I know it's awful. Those terrible people hurting children should be stopped, and the little ones should be loved and cared for. But there's nothing I can do about it."

Do you think Jesus cares about children who live on the streets? Do you believe He sees the boys and girls laboring long hours in the fields and firecracker factories? Does He identify with the pain of devastated young girls caught in the degrading life of prostitution?

He sees. He cares. He feels their pain.

Now He has given us the opportunity to see them too. The question He is asking is, How will we respond? Will we look away and steel our hearts against their pain?

I must confess that in the early years of the ministry, I was blind to these kids. Although I had been confronted by them all my life, my heart didn't break for these desperate children like it should. Then one day the Lord got my attention while I was standing at a busy street corner in a major Asian city waiting for the light to turn green.

There were little children everywhere, a common sight on busy corners throughout Asia. Tourists are cautioned not to give

Jesus said, "Let the little children come to me, and do not hinder them" (Matthew 19:14).

them anything because once you do, the others will all mob you.

While I was at this corner, feeling a bit annoyed by little hands grabbing at me, I heard from behind me the voice of a young girl.

"Sir, my father died. My mother is sick. She can't beg anymore. And I have a little brother, who is very hungry. Would you please give me a few pennies so I can buy some bread and take it to him?"

The light turned green, and everybody hurried on. But I couldn't move. What she said pierced my heart. I turned around and saw this young girl, not yet 10 years old. I will never forget her face—one of the most beautiful faces I have ever seen on a child. She had big brown eyes, thick black hair almost the length of her body, dirty fingernails, and dust mingled with sweat running down her face. She was barefoot and in rags. She just stood there with her hand extended.

I put my hands in my pocket and took out all the money I could find and gave it to her. Then I walked on.

Like the disciples on the road to Emmaus, I felt like an unseen stranger joined me on this emotional walk. The silent question He asked was deep and penetrating, "So what do you think about the little beggar girl you just met? Is her life as valuable and precious as . . ." and the face of another young girl appeared in my mind's eye. I didn't know the name of the girl on the street, but I for certain knew the name of this new face; it was my own little daughter, Sarah.

The two were approximately the same age, but their lives could not have been more contrasting. Sarah had her own carpeted room with furniture and toys and every comfort one could imagine. My wife, her German mother, made sure she was well taken care of. Her sheets and pillowcases were changed every week on her comfortable bed. She had plenty of clothes, socks, tennis shoes, a toothbrush, toothpaste, soap and shampoo. We had given Sarah all of what is so abundantly available for children born and raised in the United States.

But for the street girl I had just encountered, I doubt that she had ever held a toothbrush in her hand. Her face had never been washed with soapy water, and her hair had never been touched by shampoo. She had never slept in a warm bed under clean sheets and on fluffy pillows. Maybe she had never even heard the words, "Your mommy loves you. Your daddy loves you."

Probably her entire upbringing had been one of daily struggles—living on the streets with thousands of other children who also had no home to go to when evening came.

This question just kind of hung in the air as I walked on, "Is her life as valuable and precious as . . ."

I knew what the proper response was. Being a minister and quite familiar with the Bible, I knew right away what my answer was *supposed* to be.

"Of course, Lord! I care about her. The value of this little beggar girl's life means as much as that of my own daughter's."

No more questions were asked. I was left to process my own thoughts. What followed was one of the most difficult walks of my life. It was the first time I realized the pain and passion our Lord carries in His heart for the forgotten children in the villages and slums of these poor and destitute nations.

Honestly, I had great trouble trying to assimilate this revelation. I couldn't imagine my daughter standing on that street in Bombay with her hand out begging for a few pennies to buy a piece of bread for her brother. It was too painful for me to think about.

Yet the reality remains that the girl I met represented the faces of millions of children who are crying out not only for food, but also for help and love and hope . . . yet they can't find any.

I certainly don't want anyone to feel guilty about lovingly caring for our own children and grandchildren. But the question remains: Is there also room in our hearts for one or two of the world's millions of suffering children, and can we also care for them in Jesus' name? Can we see them as Jesus does, so special to Him, their worth like jewels beyond compare?

Are we willing to have our hearts break with His at such sights, knowing there are children who suffer so much in this life *and* have no hope of heaven in the next because they know nothing of the hope that is in Christ?

I believe, as followers of Christ, we are commanded to reach out to the least of these in the name of Jesus and show them they matter a great deal to God, who sacrificed His only Son to reach them with His love.

We must learn to look away from our own worlds to care for what God cares about. Let's not devote our energies into trinkets and mindless self-indulgence that have no eternal value, but instead learn to invest in these children God cares about so much. They truly are the least of the least—the ignored, unfed, abused and unloved. And we are told by our Lord that we cannot turn a blind eye to their plight.

SPECIAL ASSIGNMENT

Our Father in heaven is greatly concerned about the welfare of these helpless children. In fact, God has special angels assigned to watch over them at all times. Let us look again at Matthew 18:10 (NASB): "See that you do not despise one of these little ones, for I say to you that *their angels* in heaven continually see the face of My Father who is in heaven" (emphasis mine).

Now this is something very significant that Jesus is telling us here. There are angels watching over each little child in the slums, yet simultaneously, these angels are looking into the face of the Father who is sitting on the throne.

How happy these angels must be when someone feeds these

Every time a child is saved from destruction, the angels in heaven rejoice with the Father.

little children, values them, teaches them, prays for them and loves them!

This is what happened to a young lad named Nadish.

There were people who cared for him and prayed for him, and I'm sure the angels were delighted to see him set free.

This is his story.

> My mother enrolled me in a Bridge of Hope center, but I was not very interested in my studies. I preferred to play and go out at night.
>
> One day my mother said to me, "Nadish, you need to pay attention to your studies!" This made me angry.
>
> I went out that afternoon to buy some medicine for my mother. I was still unhappy and did not want

to go home, so I wandered around for a little while. I got lost near the rail station. The sun went down, and I began to get scared. I didn't recognize this place.

A nice-looking older man came by and saw that I was lost, so he offered to let me stay with him for the night.

I wish I had not gone with him.

He took me to a place far away, and before I realized what was happening, he sold me to a landlord.

The landlord forced me to clean up animal manure all day, and when I was done, he would lock me in a small room with the animals. I soon learned to ignore the smell.

Days turned into weeks, and my stomach would continually growl. He never gave me enough to eat.

Weeks turned into months, and my body would ache. The work was hard, and there was never enough time to rest.

Months turned into years, and I began to think that this would never end. I was trapped, alone, locked in this dark place with the other animals.

Then one day something strange happened. There was another boy. He had been captured too.

He cried a lot. He, too, was hungry. He, too, never got enough rest. But it was nice to have someone to talk to. He told me about his family and how he had gotten captured. I told him about my mother. I missed her very much. I had no siblings, and my father was dead.

I told him about the Bridge of Hope center. There were people there who loved me, and there was always a meal.

We worked together at the stalls. Because there were two of us, the work was easier—not because there was any less, for our taskmaster always found more work for us, but simply because there was someone to talk to. For several months, we went on like this.

Then one night, something amazing happened. The landlord forgot to lock the door! We could hardly believe our eyes. We snuck out that night and ran as fast as our tired legs could carry us.

We made it to the police station and told them what happened. They arrested that man and freed five other boys.

I was then reunited with my mother. She cried a lot when she saw me, always saying, "I was hoping some day you would be back."

I asked her if I could go back to the Bridge of Hope center. I'll be starting back very soon.

It feels so nice to wear a clean pair of clothes! To eat a full meal! To take a bath and be washed! I can smile and laugh again.

I still am scared of the dark, and I don't like to go out at night. I keep thinking this is all a dream, that one day I will wake up in that room again, but so far that has not happened.

I found out that the people at the Bridge of Hope center were praying for me. They had been for two years.

I do not know, but maybe that is why the man forgot to lock the door.

How happy the angels in heaven must have been to see Nadish free and behold his joy in the face of the Father!

Throughout Matthew and the other Gospels, we see how Jesus repeatedly highlights how important children are to Him. His heart is very close to them. He wants us to know that "when you embrace My children, you embrace Me. To touch them is to touch Me."

A Heart Like His

If you are a parent, you understand this sentiment. Who doesn't take it extremely personally when someone treats their child with special kindness? On the flip side, what parent wouldn't experience an explosive fury to learn that their child had been abused?

Close your eyes and just imagine it was *your* child who was gagged and bound and whose eyes were blinded by boiling oil. Picture *your* daughter trapped in a cage with lines of men outside. If your heart doesn't start pounding with an adrenaline rush, there is something wrong with you.

Our Lord's whole life is summarized in His mission statement, "I came to seek and save that which was lost" (see Luke 19:10). He gave Himself completely for others. Matthew 8–9 covers a period of His intense, nonstop ministry. After days of pouring Himself tirelessly into people who were suffering emotional pain, physical sickness and demon possession, the writer Matthew relates that Jesus was "moved with compassion" for the people He was seeing (see Matthew 9:36, NKJV). To Jesus, the people looked like sheep without a shepherd—hurting and lost with no one to care for them.

Matthew wrote his Gospel 30 years after the event. What do you think he must have seen in Jesus' expressions that would have been so memorable that he would record this impression so many years later?

Quite possibly, Jesus had been acting like someone who just learned of the death of a son, daughter, husband or mother. He may have been completely overcome by emotion, weeping, and He may have even lost his appetite. Maybe His legs crumbled under Him so that He could hardly stand.

Why do we picture Jesus as a stoic? Surely when He saw His own creation—the work of His hands, the people He made in His own image—being destroyed and abused, it grieved Him deeply. His heart must have felt like it was about to break. And Matthew records 30 years later: "We saw it."

It seems, though, that Jesus mourned alone. Matthew doesn't say, "We were moved by compassion too." Maybe the disciples' hearts were hard and could not feel the pain of the suffering multitude.

Jesus closed up His earthly ministry with the words, "As the Father has sent me, I am sending you" (John 20:21). We are sent into the world to show His love, but we cannot show His love until we have His heart.

God is grieved over the plight of children in this generation—children who, this very moment, are suffering in circumstances we don't even want to imagine. He is looking for individuals who will say no to themselves and instead care for the things on His heart, individuals who will tell these kids that Jesus loves them and will embrace them in His name.

Although these children are rejected and despised by their society, God sees them the same way He sees us: precious beyond compare.

Like me, I am sure that when you hear about the suffering of these downtrodden children, their parents and their families, you want to change their circumstances. You want to comfort them in their pain.

I feel sad about those early days when I didn't see these lost children the same way I saw my own. I was blinded by my own agenda, so busy in the ministry that I couldn't see the face of Christ in theirs. But then God in His mercy helped me identify with His heart for those who have no voice.

And now my prayer, like many before me, is that the Lord would break my heart with the things that break His.

"I realized that God loves me, and I also have started to love me. I thank God who has brought me so far."

—Talan, Bridge of Hope student

The first question that the priest . . . and the Levite asked was: "If I stop to help this man, what will happen to me?" But the Good Samaritan . . . reversed the question: "If I do not stop to help this man, what will happen to him?"

Martin Luther King, Jr.[1]

CHAPTER FOUR

WINDS OF CHANGE

"Give me liberty, or give me death!" is the famous proclamation by the American patriot Patrick Henry. This is the heart's cry of every human being. And who among the free would desire that others should suffer oppression, abuse or hurt?

We ache inside when we hear about the awful suffering of starving children at refugee camps and in disaster zones. It troubles us when we read about Adolf Hitler's concentration camps. We can't forget the images of thousands of helpless people—mothers, fathers, old and young—all crammed together behind electric fences. Their bodies are skin and bones, their eyes sunken with despair. Worse than seeing the pictures is knowing that many of these victims were forced into gas chambers. It makes us both angry and terribly sad.

In his book *Roots,* Alex Haley describes the plight of African people who were packed into slave ships, sent to America and sold like animals in the market. This was despicable. We ask ourselves, "How could human beings do such things to their fellow man?"

Look at the French Revolution and how the people got fed up with tyranny. In 1789, they set about to stop it. And the oppression that occurred in Romania is a more recent example of a population that suffered tremendous abuse until they wouldn't stand for it any longer. As generations had done before, they too worked for liberation. These shifts in social order are all proof that no matter how powerful a government or system becomes, people will not put up with such ill treatment forever.

In each of these cases, there came a time when someone said, "Enough!" A revolution started—some violent, others more peaceful—and soon had the support of all those with eyes open to see the plight of the suffering masses. Few people simply stood by and watched once they realized there was something they could do to help.

God steps in to save those who are suffering. To free the children of Israel from the slavery they had been under, He subjected their Egyptian slave masters to awful punishments, culminating in the death of every firstborn in that powerful empire.

The worst, most pervasive form of slavery that exists in our time is the caste system under which millions of Dalits and OBCs suffer. No other people alive today have been mistreated for as long as they have. Now they are finally saying, "Enough is enough!"

HOPE ON THE HORIZON

Today, after endless years of bondage, winds of change are blowing on the Indian subcontinent. In the late 1990s, a grassroots Dalit human rights movement started to challenge the dictates of caste segregation. This movement birthed the hope of freedom in the hearts of many Dalits and OBCs. Leaders emerged from this massive group of 750 million people to seek out justice.

These new Dalit leaders realized that the only way for them to escape the oppression they were under was to embrace faiths that would give them dignity and value and bring hope to their children. They wanted a religion that saw all human beings as equals.

The turning point came on November 4, 2001. On that day, tens of thousands of Dalits gathered in Delhi for a history-making meeting in which they publicly declared their desire to follow faiths of their own choosing. I was humbled to be invited to speak as one of the few representatives of the Church. The night spent in anticipation prior to the rally is one I will never forget.

The streets were packed, though thousands were prevented from coming because of the upper-caste opposition. These people stopped

Many Dalit leaders recognize that in order to break the bonds of caste, children will need more than just a good education; they will have to embrace a religion that views all humans as equals.

many Dalits from entering into Delhi for the freedom rally. Despite this, tens of thousands of people were able to attend, and each one was eagerly looking for hope. I was excited to be a part of it.

I remember my words as I stood before these masses who had been exploited for so long: "My precious brothers and sisters, I come to you today speaking on behalf of Christ, His love and His mercy for us all. Jesus came to set the captives free. He Himself said that 'whoever the Son sets free is free indeed.' . . . We love you with Christ's love, unconditionally and always."

This is what Jesus offers when He says, "I have come that they may have life" (John 10:10).

To grasp their logic in seeking new faiths, it's important to understand the traditional belief in reincarnation. That is, how a person lived their previous life determined the outcome of this one, including the caste into which he or she was born. For someone to be born as a Dalit basically means they were terrible in their previous life and this is their time to suffer the consequences.

This explains the shame and ill treatment heaped upon them; many Dalits genuinely believe abuse is their proper due. But if one should stop believing in reincarnation, the chains of fatalism will be broken.

That is what has happened in the hearts of millions of Dalits in the past decade. In spite of a violent backlash against their liberation, I believe a corner has been turned and major change is inevitable.

GFA wanted to offer help to the Dalits during this time of enormous transition. The greatest need among these poorest peoples of southern Asia, their leaders declared, was for their children to become educated. Simply knowing how to read would go a long way to protect them from being cheated in written contracts. It would open doors to better jobs with higher pay. This would allow them to finally get out of debt, which would end the cycle of bonded labor.

Unfortunately, the reality is not so simple. Centuries of oppression, nationwide poverty and the constant teachings of inequality are not so easy to overcome. We understood that a good education alone would not be enough to bring immediate economic and emotional healing. They need education, and they need the truth. And when they know the truth, they shall be set free (see John 8:32).

Massive Obstacles

Most Asian countries have policies that aim at making free primary education available to all children, including Dalits. For many reasons, however, they rarely attend school. The main problem is poverty. Many of these families simply cannot survive without the income their children make. If they were to go to school during the day, there would be no food for them to come home to. Bonded-labor contracts effectively kill any chance for education. Also, government schools are often too far away for the children to reach by foot.

The truth is that free education isn't really free anyway. There are fees, plus books and school supplies that are needed. Proper clothing is expected too. All of these requirements cost too much for most poor families. According to one of our social workers who ministers to slum children, most of them have only a single change of clothes. He says, "When we tell them to bathe and change their dress, they can't. So they will go home and wash, but the next day they will come in the same dress."

Although education is supposed to be free, many parents can't even afford the supplies their children need in order to attend school.

In addition, Dalit children who try to attend school usually find it a painful experience. Biases against Dalits and OBCs are often present in the classroom. They may be required to do tasks, like cleaning the grounds, which other children don't have to do.

There are still communities in which Dalits are not allowed to attend the same schools where upper-caste children study.

And even where Dalits are allowed in, they will typically have to sit in the back of the classroom and not participate in class activities. They are often verbally abused and are more likely than other children to receive corporal punishment. Teachers have been known to say that Dalit pupils cannot learn unless they are beaten.[2]

If a low-caste pupil has trouble learning a school subject, they don't have anyone at home to help them. Most parents were not allowed to go to school when they were young, so they themselves cannot read or write. All of these factors work together to discourage a student from persevering in their studies.

These are formidable obstacles to overcome, both economically and socially. GFA stepped out in faith to bring education within the reach of these children in crisis. We didn't realize at the time how great an impact this would have on everyone involved.

Encouraging Beginnings

One of the early attempts at running a school program was among the Banjara community. Their leader personally asked me to help educate their children. We were learning as we went, but the Lord was faithful, and those first efforts were wildly successful. Reports soon came in about the impact of the efforts in these villages.

Students were captivated by the love of God, which they heard about and received in tangible form from their teachers. They went home and talked about what they were learning, and their parents started getting excited, too.

Furthermore, these changes did not escape the notice of nearby communities. Before long, leaders in those villages asked our leaders in charge to start something for their children, too.

THE DREAM

The program was starting to grow, but I confess that I struggled with how people might respond. You see, my aspiration has always been to share the love of Jesus with others, bring together a local community of Christ and help them to grow in knowing the Lord. Many may be called to minister aid and comfort in this life, but I knew my place was to give people the opportunity to hear about God's love for them.

So before we expanded this program further, I sought the Lord with intense prayer and fasting for confirmation that this was the direction He wanted us to go. Soon, I had a dream God used to propel us forward.

In my dream, I was standing in front of a vast field looking out upon multitudes of desperate and suffering people just ready to slip into eternity. They had clearly been waiting for hope, but received none. I stood there for a while, overwhelmed at the sheer number of people. They seemed to fill endless acres continuing as far as my eyes could see.

Watching the pain and despair on their faces, I got this sudden understanding that I was looking upon the helpless multitudes Jesus spoke about in the Gospels, the times when He spoke of the weary and abused, like the Dalits of today. It was as though the Lord was telling me we had the opportunity before us to touch these people's lives and reach them with the love of Christ to bring hope for this life and the life to come.

Overcome with excitement at such an opportunity and imagining these precious suffering people being able to find hope for the present time and for eternity, I began to jump up and down with excitement.

I could see it, and I was so happy. I ran toward this field shouting, "Wow! We can do it! We can help all these people and let them know God cares; He loves them!"

As I raced toward the field with all my might, I was already thinking about the ways we could bring hope to these people, just like we had done for others in the past.

But something was wrong.

I suddenly couldn't go any farther. Right in front of me was a river so wide and raging I dared not step closer or try to cross it. I had not seen it from where I had been standing before.

I just stood there in agony, thinking, *Oh my goodness. Time is running out, and I am stuck. Soon it will be too late. What am I supposed to do?*

My heart broke. Was I only going to look at these needy and suffering people but not be able to help them? I stood there weeping, feeling so helpless and full of despair.

All of a sudden there appeared before me a bridge reaching from one side of the vast river to the other. It was not a narrow bridge, but one that was very broad. It was completely filled with little children from all across Asia—poor, destitute children, like those I'd so often seen on the streets of Calcutta, Kathmandu and other Asian cities, and like the same children seen in the famous award-winning movie *Slumdog Millionaire*.

I woke from my dream and realized the Lord was speaking to me about something incredibly significant: If we follow His

The Lord showed us that we could bring hope to these poor and marginalized children and through them bring hope and aid to the whole community.

instructions, our care for these children in need will be a bridge for so many people to find the hope and relief they have been looking for.

I shared this dream with my colleagues, and together we concluded that God had given us a call to bring hope to the children of Asia. Through this "bridge of hope," children would be given an education and, at the same time, would experience the love God has for all people. The extent of the opportunity was overwhelming, but knowing the Lord was behind it was all the motivation we needed.

HOPE IN CRISIS

By providing quality education to the poorest of the poor, we enable them to rise above the oppression they have lived in for centuries. And the positive response from the downtrodden is often overwhelming. Not only are the lives of children completely transformed by the simple love of Christ, but their families also are being touched and finding hope.

From my experience, I have seen that the message a child hears growing up can affect them all through their lives, whether they are encouraged to succeed or told they are worthless. My trust in the Lord began when I was a small child. My wife was the same way. The knowledge that He loved us stabilized our lives and prepared us to face the future. I am sure you can recognize in your own life how the things you learned when you were young affected the way you saw yourself and the world as you grew up.

The book of Proverbs teaches us that if you instruct a child in the way he should go, he will not depart from it when he is old (see Proverbs 22:6). If we bring these children the message of God's love for them, teaching them that they have great value in His eyes and are not limited by the caste into which they were born, they will be enabled to do great things with their lives.

I have heard it said that liberation comes through education. And this is exactly what is happening in the lives of students in GFA's Bridge of Hope Program. This is the liberation needed for the masses who live in Asia.

Many business analysts today are talking about the strong economic growth on the Indian subcontinent. The sad reality is that although the region as a whole is getting richer, the wealth is becoming increasingly concentrated in the hands of the educated minority, the high-castes who can afford to send their children to school and to college. You will almost never see a Dalit on a plane heading to the United States or to Germany to study information technology or to get an advanced degree as a lawyer, doctor or engineer. The vast majority of them are still working in the fields and factories.

This is why Bridge of Hope is so important. Education enables these children to become leaders and strong, upstanding citizens, people who will be able to serve and lead their country in the years to come. Through education, liberty won't be limited to the hands of the few.

I heard the story of one young girl who is quickly blossoming into a brilliant student and leader, although she grew up in a situation that could only be described as critical. Without the

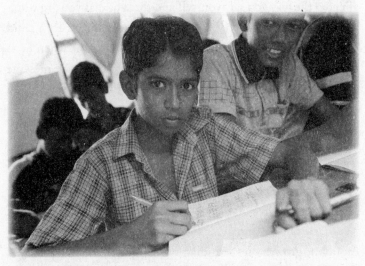

Armed with the knowledge that they have great value in the eyes of their loving Creator, these children can break the chains that have enslaved them all their lives.

intervention of the Lord through Bridge of Hope, it is hard to know what would have happened to her.

My name is Angeline. My mother was sick when I was born. I remember seeing her in her bed with big, big sores all over her body. She was always in pain. My father left us and married someone else. And then my mother died. I was 4 years old when this happened.

My grandmother decided she would take care of me, and she did until she also died when I was 6. I could not express the sorrow that I felt.

My aunt and her husband then decided to take me in. I lived in their home with their two children. It was a small room for all five of us, and we often only ate once in the day. I was so very sad then. I used to keep mum. I would not talk to anyone.

I was so scared and very sad when my aunt became sick too. I was certain that she would die and leave me.

Then something different happened. A man came and prayed for my aunt, and she got better. She decided to follow the Lord Jesus and enrolled me in a Bridge of Hope center.

When I first came, I would not talk to anybody. I would just sit in the corner by myself.

But eventually my heart was warmed. I saw the love of the people there. The women at the center were so nice and would always show me kindness.

I learned many new things at this center. My favorite verse in the Bible is James 1:5, where God says that whoever lacks wisdom should ask Him for it. So I ask God for wisdom, and He gives it to me. I started to do well in school, and now I get the best grades in my class.

I also love the Bible stories, like David and Goliath, and singing songs.

I know that I have changed a lot. I was so quiet when I came, but now I love to share with the other children—especially the ones who are quiet or hurting.

I feel so special to know that God loves me, and I pray to Him often. I pray for the Bridge of Hope center. I pray for people who are traveling, but most of all, I pray for all the people who are sick.

When I grow up, I want to tell other people about Jesus. I want to share Him with the ones who are hurting or alone or poor and sick. He has changed my life, and I want Him to change other people's lives too.

The Lord rescued Angeline, and I have no doubt that she will someday be a great and godly woman. Those who run the Bridge of Hope center say she has excellent leadership potential. This girl who was not in school only a few years prior is now excelling tremendously, and her grades are some of the best in the class. She regularly shares the love of God with many other children in her village. Angeline's dreams are great, and with the knowledge that Jesus loves her, there is no telling where her impact will end.

As I was writing this chapter, my assistant sent me a link to a story that appeared in a major Asian newspaper. The story shocked me to tears.

On January 7, 2011, more than 50 women from a rural village got together to sell their children at the market. First I thought it was a misprint. People go to market to sell vegetables and material things, not to sell their *children!* As I read on, however, I learned that their entire village is impoverished. None of these women were able to care for their children anymore. The article continued:

> Among the women was Malati Hembram who had lined up with her five-year-old daughter. "I will sell her off at whatever price I get. The money is not important; I just want my daughter to be taken in by a family which will give her food, shelter and education. We are not being able to sustain ourselves as well as our children and the elders in the family," Malati said.[3]

I don't know if any of these women actually sold their children. If someone offered these mothers money, I think they would have done so. Sadly, I read on that it is not an uncommon sight to see women going door-to-door trying to find a buyer for their son or daughter.

I have seen many stories of deprivation, misery and hopelessness, but this one caught me completely unprepared. Immediately, I called the field leader nearest to this village. I told him, "Please, set up a center in this village right away."

Within one week, I got a call back from this leader saying that they had established a Bridge of Hope center with 150 of these desperately hungry, needy children. They distributed blankets and met some basic needs of the poor people in the village. And now these children would be cared for, get a hot meal each day and receive an education. As often happens, a door was opened to share God's love and bring the assurance that He will take care of them. Thank God that we were able to learn about the situation in this village before it was too late.

God knows. He hears. He sees their pain. And He has brought us to the point at which we can, by His grace, help do something about it.

"We were reminded of our duty towards the poor after reading *No Longer a Slumdog* and *Revolution in World Missions*. We were challenged to think beyond ourselves and give someone in need a chance for a real future and hope."

—Mr. and Mrs. J.W.,
Child sponsors,
Carberry, Manitoba

*H*ow far that little candle throws his beams! So shines a good deed in a naughty world.

William Shakespeare, *The Merchant of Venice*[1]

$\mathcal{I}$T IS $\mathcal{H}$APPENING

An illiterate man came with a strange request to the leader of a GFA-supported Bridge of Hope center. Would they send the "medical doctor named Jesus" to help his sick wife? He was dead serious and quite desperate in his pleading.

Here is the story. In this Bridge of Hope center, a first grader named Nibun was getting the opportunity to receive an education in mathematics, reading and writing. He also heard stories about how Jesus healed the sick, cast out demons and fed the hungry.

Nibun's home was a mud hut where he lived with his parents. Like other poor families, they didn't have the luxury of going to a hospital when they were sick; it was simply too expensive, and most doctors were several miles away. Five or ten miles may not seem like much while riding in a car or a bus, but it's a long distance to travel on a dirt path through the woods, especially when sick.

Nibun's mother had been very ill. His father did everything he could and even cried out to all his deities for help. But she continued to get worse, and soon her situation became critical. That's when Nibun told his father about the amazing things Jesus did. And this poor man thought there was a medical doctor named Jesus at the Bridge of Hope center.

In response to his request, two workers went to extend whatever help they could. Often social workers provide hope and tools to help families with their particular needs. These workers talked with the family about God's love for them and His mercy. They also laid hands on the woman and prayed God would heal her in Jesus' name. Just as we read in God's Word, the Lord in His mercy healed her.

Through this healing, one by one, others close to Nibun's family came to understand the Lord's loving and compassionate nature. They saw how the Bridge of Hope center cared for people from low castes and reached out to help them. And when Nibun's mother was healed, they began to understand how much God loved them and that He cared to reach down and intervene in their lives. They were so thankful to God for the hope they found through this incident.

Think about it. What if Nibun had not been attending the Bridge of Hope center? Would he have been able to tell his father about the "medical doctor named Jesus" who healed his mother? Perhaps the villagers would never have realized the depth of God's love for them. Without someone reaching out to his family, would they have known there was help and hope for their situation? How many people living nearby would still not realize their value in the sight of God?

All of those touched by Nibun's mother being healed experienced a hope and a peace they had never known before. And this story of God's touch on the life of a student and his family is not an exception; it is a daily occurrence.

THEY FIND HOPE

My eyes fill with tears of joy when I think of the tens of thousands of dear children in GFA-supported Bridge of Hope centers. Through national workers who serve in these marginalized communities, children find hope in Jesus.

Beacons of life and healing, Bridge of Hope centers are facilities established in a community where up to 200 children are able to come every day. These centers provide a holistic approach to their development, focusing on three main areas: the child's physical, mental and spiritual growth.

Physical Needs

A Bridge of Hope center is tailored to meet the specific physical needs of the children attending. For example, nutrition specialists determine what food and vitamins are needed at each center and fix a daily meal accordingly. In addition, Bridge of Hope provides each child a uniform, a backpack and school supplies like pencils and books. Furthermore, as the staff observes the children, they can learn what other items the children need—things like toothpaste and towels that many of the children have either never heard of or never even considered using before.

These physical necessities were desperately needed after the devastating tsunami in 2004. It tore through South Asia, killing an estimated 200,000 people, flattening whole villages and leaving more than a million people homeless.[2]

There was a young woman named Mariyam whose life was almost destroyed by the monster waves. Before it hit, her husband made a decent living selling fish. The family ate well, and

Being able to eat every day is no longer a luxury for the many children in GFA Bridge of Hope.

the children were able to attend school. But that was before he lost all his fishing boats. Without the boats, there was no income.

Her husband went to his parents for help, but they refused because Mariyam was of a lower caste than they were. When he returned home, beside himself with grief, he did the unthinkable; he committed suicide by dousing himself with kerosene and setting himself on fire.

Mariyam was left in shock. She was now a widow with a lame foot, an infant daughter, two school-age boys and no income. She did what she could to sell odds and ends but only made about 30 cents a day. The family was not surviving.

That's when the Lord sent a sister from the local fellowship to visit her. She shared the love of Christ, and Mariyam, hearing there was a God who loved her in the midst of this suffering, received Jesus into her heart. She started to attend the fellowship and learned about Bridge of Hope.

Her sons were admitted into the local Bridge of Hope center, where their tuition was paid and they received help with their studies. They were also fed a wholesome meal every day, which was something their mother wasn't able to provide. Because the boys had no father, the staff at the center took special care of them. For the first time in their lives, the two brothers heard songs and stories about Jesus. Now the whole family has drawn close to the Lord.

Healthy Living

Part of the curriculum taught at the centers is on health and hygiene. Children are taught the importance of washing their hands after using the facilities and before they eat, as well as taking a bath regularly. Every year they get a medical checkup. This is the first time many of these children have seen a doctor.

As we sit in our homes with indoor plumbing, central air and plenty of blankets, it's hard to imagine how the simple act of bathing can have an eternal impact on someone's life. But that's exactly what happened in one Bridge of Hope center.

At that center, there were two unruly boys named Deepan and Chitral. Although their father was opposed to the Christian faith, he still enrolled his children in the center so they could get an education. This family was poor and knew almost nothing about hygiene. Because of this, the two brothers had sores all over their bodies when they first came to the center.

The Bridge of Hope staff started to bathe the boys with warm water. They talked to the parents about hygiene, but they did not want to listen. Nevertheless, the staff would apply medicine and dress the boys' sores. Through this care and prayer, the boys were healed.

As time went by, Deepan and Chitral became more disciplined, and their parents took notice. At home, the brothers would sing songs they learned at the center. They would pray before meals and prior to studying.

Both their father and mother were amazed. Gradually their hearts opened to the love of God, and now they are learning more about Him regularly. This story is not uncommon; there are many parents, neighbors and relatives whose lives have changed as a result of a Bridge of Hope center being present in their village.

Academic Excellence

Year after year, the children from Bridge of Hope consistently get high marks in their classes. There are Bridge of Hope students who achieve first rank and first class. Bridge of Hope students are regularly among the highest-scoring children in the state of Nepal and throughout India. How does this happen?

The students at Bridge of Hope centers learn good study habits from the teachers who work with them. They have adequate time to ask questions, get tutoring and learn how to think creatively. Children are encouraged to pray for wisdom and understanding in their schooling. Thus they improve in school and receive higher marks on their exams. This boosts their confidence and encourages them to keep attending.

One young lad named Ghalib was an unruly child who disobeyed and found it difficult to concentrate on anything. He would fight with his parents even as they would fight with each other.

Then his mother found out about Bridge of Hope and enrolled Ghalib, forcing him to attend. In his own words, he "found something new."

Through the attentive tutelage he received, he learned to pay attention to his studies and began to succeed in school. He also learned about the love of Jesus and started to value his new opportunity. He has memorized Psalm 23 by heart and often prays to the Lord. When asked about his experience, Ghalib said, "Really, God has blessed my family and me."

Lessons for Life

In addition to the lessons about discipline and study, the children also learn moral values such as the importance of respecting parents and elders, of telling the truth and of not being willfully disobedient. This transformation in attitude and behavior is quickly noticed by parents.

Padimni's parents came to the local Bridge of Hope center to thank the teachers for the change they saw in their daughter. The girl had been a thief most of her life, often stealing food from her family and money from her father. But one day at the center, she heard about Jesus, and it changed her completely. Padimni listened carefully to a lesson taught about stealing. She learned that stealing was wrong and that she should change her behavior. So she did.

Another child, a boy named Isar, was constantly fighting with the neighboring boys. His parents warned him that he wouldn't have any friends because of his actions. And they were right; Isar found himself without any friends.

Then he met two new boys who were enrolled in a Bridge of Hope center nearby. They befriended him, even though he was

Children learn vital skills such as discipline, hygiene and manners. They become more respectful and courteous and are more willing to study and help their parents at home.

an angry child. He asked his mother if he could go to the center too, so she enrolled him.

The changes in Isar were swift and dramatic. His parents didn't hear complaints about his negative behavior anymore. Isar made many friends and learned to respect his parents and his elders. His whole nature and attitude changed.

Spiritual Lessons

One of the most amazing things to hear about is how God is revealing Himself to these children. As they encounter His love at the centers, the Holy Spirit works in the hearts of these young ones, showing them God's faithfulness. It is beautiful to see children offer up their prayers to the Lord and to witness their joy at His amazing responses.

Rinvi is a perfect example. This young girl was more interested in hearing about Jesus than in playing games. She would remember the details of all the stories she heard.

Her grandfather, who lived with her family, could not see. They had tried everything they could, including an operation, but nothing helped. Then one day Rinvi remembered a story about a blind man whom Jesus healed. Because of this, she believed the Lord was also able to heal her grandfather.

When she got home that day, she boldly told her grandfather that the Lord was able to heal him. Then she asked him to close his eyes, and she prayed for him to be healed. As she prayed, he regained his eyesight.

After this miracle, Rinvi's faith began to grow. One day she was stuck at the Bridge of Hope center because of heavy rains, so she prayed for the rain to stop. And it did.

Another girl, Madhari, wanted God to heal her dad because he had been vomiting for two days. She prayed for him, and God healed him!

Then there was a little boy named Balaji; he was only 5 years old!

At his Bridge of Hope center, he heard stories about God's miraculous healings. So when he and his friend both caught a fever, he prayed that night to be healed so he could go back to school. The next morning he woke up in perfect health and was surprised that his friend was still sick! So later that night Balaji told his buddy that he needed to ask Jesus for his healing too.

It amazes me how beautifully simple the faith of these children is. God said it, so it must be true. They memorize Scriptures, whole psalms and chapters, as well as action songs and Bible stories.

The children learn to pray at Bridge of Hope, and it is beautiful to see how God answers their requests time and time again. Their faith in Him grows as He heals the sick, changes lives and performs miracles.

Children learn by the example they see, and when given a good example to follow, they will take it and run with it. This is what happened in one Bridge of Hope center.

Sagen is an 8-year-old boy who lives in a poor village where there is no electricity. Most of the people there labor in the fields around their homes.

At the center where Sagen attends, the children frequently see the staff praying about various matters. The staff also encourages the children to pray for each other. They have formed prayer groups and can be seen almost every day, whether in school or out, praying for each other's needs. Sagen is the leader of one such group that has attained quite the reputation.

Sagen and several other children found out about a boy named Santanu Malik, who had been sick for several years. He lived in the next village over. The boy's mother was so distressed about his illness that she thought, *If I can, I'll go inside the earth or I'll go above the sky to flee from this situation.*

Her son had a tumor in his brain that left him unable to walk. Sometimes the right side of his body would twitch violently, and he wasn't able to eat much. Sagen and the boys visited Santanu many times to pray for him, but nothing seemed to be happening. Still they persisted. Then one day Santanu was suddenly healed! He even went outside to play with his new friends.

Since then, Sagen and his young "prayer partners" have been called on to pray for many other people in the village. When Sagen's grandfather became ill with stomach pains, he simply said, "Sagen, you know how to pray. Would you please pray for me?" The next day his grandfather told him, "Because of your prayers, I got healed."

It has gotten to the point that whenever anyone in the village gets sick, they call for the boys on this prayer team. God is using these boys' prayers to open up many hearts to Himself.

Sagen continues to pray because as he puts it, "Really, it's so amazing to speak with the Creator of all! And when we pray to Jesus, we feel good in our hearts."

I am overwhelmed when little children like this are open and responsive to God's work in their hearts! No wonder Jesus said, "I tell you the truth, unless you change and become like little children, you will never enter the kingdom of heaven" (Matthew 18:3). We have much to learn from these young ones.

Families Flourish

Parents of the children in our Bridge of Hope centers often tell us of amazing things that happen in their homes through their kids. The children act as the conduit of God's love, teaching their parents what they have learned.

Here is the story of one such family that was changed by their son's involvement in a Bridge of Hope center. The boy's father, Rajiv, relates what happened.

After attending the Bridge of Hope center, my son used to come home and say, "This is what my sir said, and this is what our teacher taught us." Regarding spiritual life, regarding our way of living and regarding our health and hygiene, he would come and tell us. It was kind of exciting! So, when my son says something to me, for example, about hygiene, I am changing.

Some of the things he says about prayer and about Jesus really touch me. Slowly by slowly, I am changing according to what he says to us.

The Bridge of Hope really brought a kind of revival in me spiritually. Basically I'm an illiterate person. I do not know how to read and write. Many times my son would come and say words he learned at the Bridge of Hope center. "This is what the Word of God says." So many times when we would do wrong things, the Word of God would speak to us. And because it was the Word of God speaking, we changed a lot.

We have prayer every day in our home for 15 to 20 minutes. My son reads the Bible, and we sing some songs. Now Jesus is the main focus of our life. We cannot leave Jesus and go anywhere, because Jesus is with us and He guides us every day. This kind of spiritual awareness, through my son, I got through Bridge of Hope.

Children aren't the only ones who are transformed. Their parents watch their conduct and learn of the Lord from them, and their lives are also impacted. I remember hearing of one little boy named Ruhan and how the Lord intervened in the lives of his parents and saved them from making a terrible decision.

Ruhan showed up at his Bridge of Hope center one morning in tears, having just learned that his parents were going to file for divorce that very day. He poured out his heart to one of the staff members. When they realized what was going on, the leader and the social worker at the center rushed to the courthouse to do some last-minute marital counseling.

Because of problems they were having, Ruhan's parents had decided to divorce. The two staff members were able to counsel them and to help them understand the importance of restoring their broken marriage, not only for themselves but also for their son.

Through the intervention, prayers and counseling of the staff, Ruhan's parents recommitted themselves to accept each other and live together.

As they learned more about Christ, his parents' hearts knit back together. Now they have a strong marriage, and the whole

Children take their
newfound joy home
with them and share it
with their parents.

family is growing in the saving knowledge of the Lord. His peace
in their lives is evident to all.

COMMUNITY DEVELOPMENT

Like with Nibun, the little boy whose father thought Jesus
was a doctor, the healing touch of a Bridge of Hope center ex-
tends into the whole community. The children individually take
home what they have learned to their parents, and the staff open
up the center and invite people in as well.

The trained staff is able to help villagers struggling with issues such as alcoholism and family strife. Through prayer and counsel, entire villages have been transformed. No longer places of hopelessness, these villages are filled with joyful, caring people who finally have a reason for living.

GFA-supported programs work together with Bridge of Hope to bless the community in numerous ways. A center may offer workshops open to everyone on a health care issue or put on a presentation for a holiday. Bridge of Hope centers also sponsor "community days" in which the staff goes out and cleans the village gutters and bus stops.

GFA supporters fund "Jesus Wells" that provide pure water for those who would otherwise have to walk great distances or for people denied access because of their caste. There are literacy programs, vocational training and micro-financing, all to enable poor men and women to escape the poverty and oppression in which they have been trapped for several millennia.

GFA-supported medical clinics are often attended by the entire village. There are so many who need help that sometimes people stand in line all day just to be seen!

GFA also has a catalog we put out every Christmas with various items like sewing machines, water filters, goats, chickens and rickshaws that people with financial means can buy to help people in Asia. The social workers at Bridge of Hope centers know the poor families in their communities who would most benefit from the free gift of a cow or a fishing net. These items show Christ's love in a tangible way, while they are also tools to help break the cycle of poverty that is so prevalent in Dalit and low-caste communities.

Within all of these programs, we have seen that helping kids is the largest bridge to bring hope to a family, a village or a people.

The staff of the Bridge of Hope centers are able to counsel the parents, as was the case with the boy Ruhan, and give them a new perspective on life. Health is improved as villagers learn about sanitation, like with Deepan and Chitral. The prayers of the children are answered by the Almighty God, as He heard the cries of Rinvi, Balaji and Sagen. Children like Padimni and Isar blossom into well-behaved students who excel in their studies. Each one of these children impacted their community and is a testimony to the transformational power of the Lord.

As people come to know the Lord and experience life as He offers it, communities are transformed. There is grace, there is peace and there is a supernatural love that people have for one another. Even members of warring communities who have been engaged in bloody conflicts for as long as anyone can remember are sitting together to worship the Lord in unity.

It is impossible to tell the full extent of what the Lord is doing in Asia today; there is no one person who knows all of it! However, the events going on in one area provide a glimpse into the awesome work of the Lord.

When GFA-supported workers first went to this community, they were struck with the hopelessness and oppressive atmosphere in which the people lived. The children were uneducated, hardly dressed and sick from easily preventable causes like having no clean water to drink and a vitamin deficiency. The parents and their children toiled all hours of the day, and when there wasn't any work, they went hungry. Many of the men would come home and abuse their wives and children, wasting their money on drugs and alcohol. They knew nothing of the genuine love of Christ.

For the past several years, GFA has been showing Christ's love to these hurting people. GFA-supported workers began visiting families, listening to their struggles and offering prayer and counsel. We also helped provide Jesus Wells, open Bridge of Hope centers, extend one-day medical clinics to the community and begin literacy programs for the women, basically doing all that we could to be a blessing to these people and help them better survive the harsh circumstances into which they were born.

The people here saw how hard we tried to be of help and to love them in the midst of the depravity in which they lived. For the first time, their children got an education, and their mothers learned how to read. Husbands who used to be drunkards and abusive to their families became decent, honest men. Many of the families here came to know the love of Christ and decided to follow Him! There was a renewing of their minds, their hearts were warmed toward each other, and the people started to care for others, not just themselves. It is simply astounding to see what God has done in this one community alone!

At first, they wanted to know, "Why are you doing this? What is it about your God that would cause you to help us?" Now, as they experience God's love in their own lives, they are beginning to see it flow out of them, too.

These stories have been repeated over and over. By the grace of God, there are so many testimonies like this. Physical assistance alone cannot account for the amazing transformation in people's lives. There is only one way we can explain it: *God is working in people's hearts.*

It Is Happening

Lift up your eyes. Children are being fed, clothed and loved. They are getting an education like no one in their family ever did before. Thousands of them are experiencing the love of Christ. There are more than 75,000 children enrolled in Bridge of Hope centers (as of 2015), which we are grateful for, but what is that number compared to the millions who are still wandering without hope?

So many people are now open to the message of love found in the Good News. The need is almost overwhelming. The sheer numbers drive us to our knees. But don't be daunted by the size of the task; you *can* make a difference in the life of a child.

In some parts of the world, when the tide comes in from the ocean, it brings with it thousands of starfish. Then the tide recedes and leaves thousands of them behind on the shore. Many of these starfish cannot make it back to the safety of the water before the sun comes up and dries them out.

A man was walking along the shore one day and witnessed this sight. He stared at all the starfish, saddened that so many would die.

Then he saw a young boy walking in the other direction. The lad would stop and pick up a starfish and throw it into the ocean. He continued to do this, picking up one after the other and throwing them back into the water.

"Why are you doing that?" the man asked the boy. "Don't you realize there are miles and miles of shore? You're wasting your time. You'll never make a difference."

The boy simply picked up another starfish and hurled it back into the ocean. As it landed, he said, "I made a difference for that one."

Like the young boy, we cannot save them all. But you and I *can* make a difference. Let's not let what we can't do stop us from doing what we can do.

"I see the faces of these precious children and my heart goes out to them. I like to think that one person can make a difference, even if it is only one child at a time."

—Ms. M.L.,
Child sponsor,
Saltsburg, Pennsylvania

Every man feels instinctively that all the beautiful sentiments in the world weigh less than a single lovely action.

James Russell Lowell[1]

CHAPTER SIX

W<small>HAT</small> N<small>OW</small>?

A few years ago while speaking at a conference in Los Angeles, I talked about the plight of the suffering Dalits and the hopelessness of their children. Some of the statistics shocked my audience, such as the fact that more than 1.2 million children are trafficked as slaves and prostitutes every single year.[2]

At the end of the session, a man came up to me and handed me a CD, saying, "You will want to listen to the song, 'What Now.' You'll like it." The CD was by the musician Steven Curtis Chapman.[3]

I listened to the song later that day, and his lyrics moved me to tears.

Through the song, you find yourself face-to-face with an orphaned little girl on "the other side of world," destitute, just looking at you. The Lord steps in and basically says, "I am that girl." And His question then hangs in the air: *What now?*

I must warn you, my reader—you can no longer say you didn't know. Through this book, you've seen their faces. I am sure you have felt their pain.

The question I need to ask you is—and I ask on behalf of these children and the God who cares for them—what will you do now?

Like me, I believe you want to save them. I think you've heard their pleas for help, and you hope there is something you can do to rescue them.

I want to inform you that there is a way, and you can be part of the rescue party. Please join with us as we continue to build this "bridge of hope" for the children of Asia.

The path of their life is completely changed by these children's involvement in a GFA-supported Bridge of Hope center.

It has already become evident that the Lord greatly desires to see these young lives reached, and He has given us the unique privilege to join Him in His awesome work.

PRAY

When you see these photos of children or hear the stories of what they have suffered, don't let heartbreak and compassion be the extent of your response; begin to *pray*. There is nothing so crucial to our ministry as prayer. As Sir Thomas Buxton said, "You know the value of prayer; it is precious beyond all price. Never, never neglect it."[4]

As you read in earlier chapters, God answers when His people call out to Him. Pray for the children you see and read about. If you don't know the name of a given child, make up a name. God knows whom you are speaking to Him about and will do His work to change that life.

For some time, our home office staff has been praying against the sexual assaults that happen to little girls in Asia. Our hearts were burdened whenever we prayed about this during our regular prayer meetings. Recently, we were encouraged to hear this story of how God has answered.

In Sri Lanka, there was a village of laborers who lived in shanty homes. Every night, men from the neighboring areas would come and rape the young girls. There was nothing the laborers could do to stop them. The poor workers lived in constant fear.

When a GFA-supported missionary found out about this situation, he went to the authorities. They responded, assuring protection for the people. Furthermore, they allowed the missionary, his wife and several women from the church to minister to the people of this village. They now give the children baths, trim their fingernails, feed them balanced meals and pass out clothes to wear. The Lord is working. I believe He heard our prayers for these little girls.

You too can literally change lives by praying. God is ready to answer. Remember the story of Nadish and how the Lord rescued him?

If you want ideas of what to pray for, go to our website, www. gfa.org/slumdog/pray. You will see numerous children and families to pray for. Look at their pictures. Read their stories. Listen to their songs.

Ever since we started more than 30 years ago, GFA has always been a ministry with prayer as the focus. We intercede on behalf of the lost world every Tuesday night and the first Friday of every month. Likewise, I encourage you to pray. If there is a prayer team that meets at your church, join them and add your faith to theirs. If there is not, why not start your own prayer group? Invite everyone you can, no matter their age. When we have special prayer requests, we ask the children at our home office to pray— and it happens! God answers.

I wrote a brochure about how to have an effective and lively prayer meeting. This brochure, *Guidelines to Effective Prayer Meetings,* can be downloaded for free online. Please make prayer a regular part of your life and be confident that God hears and answers. You will be blessed also as you come before the Lord and seek His face.

BRING THEM HOPE

I encourage you to take yet another step and become a sponsor for one of these needy children, a young boy or girl somewhere in Asia. As you donate to GFA's Bridge of Hope Program, you will enable Bridge of Hope to provide life-changing assistance to your sponsored child, as well as to thousands of children throughout Asia. Bridge of Hope provides children with a quality education, a daily nutritious meal, medical care and a safe place to laugh, grow and experience the love of Christ, the One who transforms lives.

Instead of a future where she is forced to provide for her family through backbreaking physical labor, this child will go on to receive a higher education, becoming an engineer or possibly a teacher.

To sponsor a Bridge of Hope child, simply fill out the pre-addressed sponsorship card that is included in this book and drop it in the mail. Alternately, you can go to our website, www.gfa.org/slumdog, and prayerfully look through the pictures. God will guide you to a child.

Once you become a sponsor, you then have the incredible privilege of praying for and writing to your child. You will receive his or her prayers and letters in return. Your child will never forget you or what you have done.

Remember, too, that your chosen child will not be the only one whose life is transformed. I am constantly amazed how the Lord works not only in the hearts of individuals but also in communities, transforming many lives through a single Bridge of Hope center. As if that were not enough, the families of the people who sponsor these children are also radically changed. One by one the stories reach us, revealing God's special providence in each situation.

There were two young brothers, ages 7 and 5, who were learning about Asia. They were especially touched when they heard about the needs of many of the children there. Their parents started reading to them my first book, *Revolution in World Missions,* and the boys were eager to help in whatever way they could. Their parents showed them our website so they could get personally involved.

The boys prayed for several days, asking God to help them choose a child to sponsor. Then they spent about an hour online searching through the children until they announced they had found one. He was a boy just about their age.

In order to pay for the sponsorship, they started their own "cookie company." They have been baking them every week since. I'm told their house smells like it too! The two boys hope to make enough money to soon start sponsoring another child.

Their parents have said, "What a blessing it is to see God working in the hearts of our own children as they reach out to serve others."

SPREAD THE WORD

We can all learn from the example of these two young boys. In order to sell their cookies, I imagine they have had opportunities to tell their extended family and neighbors about their sponsored child.

Likewise, you can be a part of the rescue team by spreading the word. This book is an excellent resource to open people's eyes to this reality, and you can order more copies to give to your friends or relatives.

We have other books as well. If you haven't already, I encourage you to read my first book, *Revolution in World Missions.* It tells of the origins of GFA and the work of our national missionaries. You can order a copy at www.gfa.org.

But don't stop with your immediate family; share what you are doing with your friends, relatives, co-workers and church members. Explain why you are doing it and how they too can get involved.

SIMPLE LIVING

Many people find the idea of sponsoring a child to be an incredible eye-opener. They come to appreciate the blessings they have and start to recognize that they own much more than they need. Just the cost of coffee, of going out to eat, of the latest fashions, T-shirts, CDs and DVDs, or even of that special candy you love so much can literally save a child in Asia.

Often I go through my closet and remove all the clothes I don't wear. I don't need them. I drive around in a 1962 yellow

Volkswagen bug—it still works! I remember in the early days of the ministry when God convicted me about how much money I spent on chewing gum.

Please don't misunderstand. I'm not saying that a nice car or new clothes or anything like that is a bad thing. If poverty made us more spiritual, then there would be a lot of really spiritual people all over Asia. No. This is about seeing the little ways that the Lord calls us to live simply so that others might simply live.

God reveals to people all over the world about the small sacrifices they can make in His name. In one instance, there was a mother who used to spend $30 every month to buy a special makeup she loved. She knew in her heart that it was only a fleeting thing, and she wanted to invest in something with eternal value. The Lord had been telling her family to die to the cares of this world and to take up their cross and follow Him. So they did, and He led them to support a Bridge of Hope child. Together with her two sons, ages 7 and 9, she picked out a child to sponsor and pray for. Her boys even gave $2, the only money they had. As they pray together and write to their child, it's been a great way to bond as a family.

I recall another family that downgraded their cable subscription so that they could sponsor two children. Their hope was to teach their own children to enjoy giving more than receiving. They could honestly say, "What a difference [GFA] is making in the lives of children . . . including our own."

One little girl gave "lots of money" to sponsor another young girl in Asia. Her words were, "I am almost 5 years old, and I saw the little children who had no clothes, food, dolls or anything and had to dig in the garbage. So I got out lots of money to give to them. I want them to have a doll of their own. I love the little girl I saw."

Perhaps because these children are still so young, they can empathize with someone who has lost their mother or wonder what it would be like not to have food to eat or toys to play with. And they have not learned to ignore what they see.

The words of one girl changed the course of someone on the other side of the world, and she was only 3 years old. Her parents heard about GFA's Christmas catalog while listening to a spot on the radio. They came to our website, www.gfa.org/gift, to give a goat. Then they got a copy of my first book, and their eyes were opened to our national missionary program, so they sponsored three missionaries. After that, they found out about GFA's Bridge of Hope Program.

Soon, they sat with their young daughter in front of the computer, looking through the children's pictures. The parents chose to sponsor a little boy. Then they continued to look further through the profiles. That's when their little daughter spoke up and pointed to a young girl. Her parents clicked on her, and their daughter laughed and smiled, saying, "Now we have picked a boy and a girl!"

Her parents had not intended to sponsor two children that night. So they asked their little daughter, "Which one should we sponsor, the boy or the girl?"

She said, "Both of them." And they could think of no reason why not to.

Our Privilege

You know the need, the opportunity and the urgency. What now? I pray you will not say, "I need to think about it," or "I'm too busy right now. I'll do it later," or a dozen other excuses.

Procrastination is a deadly enemy. We mean well. We may know we are prompted by God to do something, but somehow we forget about it. Our lives become busy, and somehow our "good intentions" drop to the bottom of our to-do lists.

But there is something you can do right now to bring hope to the least of these: pray, spread the word and sponsor a child. Make a choice to love them as Christ does.

Please help us reach out and save these children.

A "bridge of hope" is being built one child at a time, touching the lives of people who were born into hopelessness. These are people Christ loves, people He died to save.

It's my heart's cry: *Lord, help us rescue at least 500,000 children from despair and hopelessness.* Together, we can give them hope.

Sponsoring a child is one of the most fulfilling joys. I know a doctor who traveled to the mission field and got to help conduct medical camps for Bridge of Hope centers. Dr. Daniel and his family have been impacted by the need and are blessed as a whole family to sponsor Bridge of Hope children. This is his story.

I woke up from my sleep hearing some moans and sobs from my 2-year-old daughter's bed. I checked the time; it was 2:30am. Why was she crying at this time? I got out of my bed and walked over to her room. She was sitting up in bed and softly moaning. Sitting beside her, I asked what happened. In between her sobs she pointed to her stomach and said she's hungry. I quickly realized that she had not eaten enough the previous night for dinner; she was too involved in playing with her friends that she had forgotten to complete her meal.

Half asleep, I took her downstairs and put her on her chair and went to the kitchen. I brought her favorite breakfast—milk and honey loops. Putting it in a bowl, I set it before her and just slumped on the chair. She was happy and was eagerly eating.

Suddenly a thought came to my mind. I've been blessed by God that even in the middle of the night, when my child was hungry, I had enough to give her to eat. But how many children, probably the same age or even younger, do not have the same privilege? How many children would have had to go hungry the previous night? How many parents, even if their child cried from hunger, would not have been able to give food?

What can I do about it?

My attention soon went to the wall beside my daughter, where there was a picture hanging. That was of Prabhavati—a girl, from Manipur—a north-eastern state of India. She was our Bridge of Hope child whom, as a family, we were sponsoring for the past several years. I got regular letters from my Bridge of Hope child and saw the progress she was making. Having visited several Bridge of Hope centers as a doctor conducting medical camps, I knew that these children were taken care of well. A nutritious meal each day, vitamins and basic medical check-ups at least twice a year, hygiene supplies 3 to 4 times a year, a chance at learning arts and crafts and more than that, a chance to complete basic level education—all these were things which would make sure her future was bright and full of hope.

I determined that the first thing in the morning I'd do was to sponsor two more children, one in my son's name and one in my daughter's name. The next morning I did just that. I put my 7-year-old son on my lap and showed him pictures of Bridge of Hope children who needed to be sponsored on the computer.

I said, "Just like we educate you and give you food and clothes, we are going to help another child."

He picked a kid of his own age, Sunny. Then it was my daughter's turn. She too picked up a child her age, Saraswathi from Bihar, probably the poorest state in India.

fold before tearing

Yes! I want to help children in Asia. GOSPEL FOR ASIA'S BRIDGE OF HOPE *Program*

Dear Brother K.P., after reading *No Longer a Slumdog*, I've decided I want to join with those who are helping children in need.

☐ **Starting now, I will commit to _____ monthly pledge(s)** to help children in Gospel for Asia's Bridge of Hope Program at $35 each, for a total of $ _____ per month. (For every $35 pledge, you will receive the photo and profile of a child you can link your life with. You will have the opportunity to pray for, encourage and correspond with your sponsored child(ren) in the days ahead.)

☐ **I would like to give an additional $5 per month** to help GFA gain more support for Bridge of Hope children.

Please circle: Mr.   Mrs.   Miss   Rev.

Name _____

Address _____

City _____ State _____ Zip _____

Phone ( ) _____

Email _____

☐ Get our weekly email digest, and be inspired as you see how God is transforming lives in Asia.
Privacy Policy: GFA will not sell, lease or trade your personal information.

All gifts are subject to our Gift Acceptance Policy. | gfa.org/giftpolicy

Sponsor a child who shares your birthday or the birthday of a loved one!

gfa.org/birthday

HB74-RB9C

I want to make a DIFFERENCE!

Your pledge will help provide a quality education, medical care and daily meals for children in need. It will also help these children know how much they are loved.

Your stamp on this card is like an
additional donation!—Bro. K.P.

fold before tearing

Sponsor a child, get news
from the mission field
and download free
resources at

GFA.ORG

Within a couple of days, we got their pictures and a small description of them in our mail. It was exciting as we together hung up the two children's pictures beside the other girl.

My son read his sponsored child's hobbies and said, "Papa he's just like me—likes maths and likes to play cricket! He likes drawing too!"

My daughter wasn't able to read by herself yet, but she was excited to see Saraswathi's picture too.

It's been almost 3 years since that late-night meal with my daughter. Now I have 3 children of my own and 3 children whom we sponsor. I sometimes say that I have 6 children! One of the best times we have as a family is when we get a letter from one of our Bridge of Hope sponsored children, and we sit together to read the letter and see the paintings or pictures they have sent to us. My son loves drawing and so he paints or draws a picture to send back to his sponsored child. I help my daughter to colour a picture to send back to Saraswathi. Then we say a prayer for them, for God to keep them safe and to help them study well.

The need is large; but for these 3 children, we have made a difference.

While we care for our own children, let us remember there are millions walking on the streets, homeless and helpless. There are hundreds of millions more suffering in the remote villages. They live their lives in conditions we cannot fathom. Their little hearts suffer more pain than anyone should have to bear. Many children honestly believe they are worth less than a dog.

But you can help change that. You can bring hope to a little child.

Like in the movie *Slumdog Millionaire,* these children roam the streets. That's reality.

But now there is something you *can* do about it.

Please, go before the Lord.

He will tell you what to do.

"I saw [on GFA's website] a beautiful little boy that touched my heart. I want him to have hope in his heart and know how much God loves him. God says He gives us hope and a future."

—Ms. S.S.,
Child sponsor,
Grand Prairie, Texas

*N*obody made a greater mistake than he who did nothing
because he could do only a little.

Edmund Burke[1]

CHAPTER SEVEN

MAKE YOUR LIFE COUNT

Regrets. I've had a few in my life. There are times I said to myself, "If only . . ." or "I wish . . ." Like you, I feel sad for the past failures, mistakes and sins.

One of my most painful memories has to do with a little girl named Meena. Meena was a beautiful 5-year-old living in a slum. She had the biggest brown eyes. When the social workers first saw her, she was standing in six inches of sewer water.

Meena was one of the thousands of children who survive by begging on the streets. No one knows if her parents abandoned her or simply died. Her life was sustained by the meager sums she could coax from passersby and the scraps she would often eat out of the garbage piles just to stay alive.

I saw a photo of Meena, and it's one I can never forget. Later, I learned that she began eating sewage-infested dirt off of the streets. Soon she went into a coma and died.

The sad thing is that there are still children eating dirt to fill their empty stomachs. They are silent victims of poverty, quietly passing unnoticed from some of the darkest places on earth.

For Meena it's too late. My deep regret is that there was no Bridge of Hope center in her slum to rescue her.

Children like Meena make it important, critically important, for us to move from "good intentions" to *actions*.

C.S. Lewis put it very well when he said, "The more often we feel without acting, the less we will be able ever to act, and, in the long run, the less we will be able to feel."[2]

We have now walked together through almost all the pages of this book. You have started to feel the pain and anguish of these forgotten lives. I assume your heart was touched as you read the real-life accounts of the Dalits, the OBCs and especially their precious children.

Please don't close your heart now. Don't start to numb the pain you feel for these suffering, helpless children. Please love them. Love them in Jesus' name.

You and I did not ask to be born and raised in the circumstances and comforts we have. You too could have been born destitute in a slum or in a Dalit family. You could have been that little slumdog, blinded and turned into a street beggar. It's true, you might even have been sold into the sex business and died long before your 20th birthday.

God in His mercy gave us the privilege of living our lives with the freedom and blessings words can't describe. Just remember Jesus' words: "From everyone who has been given much, much will be required" (Luke 12:48, NASB).

There is no need to feel guilt and self-condemnation for the blessings we have. Instead, let us choose to see this challenge as an opportunity to be like Jesus in our generation.

I think you will agree, once in a while God tries to break into our normal lives and tell us something important. He brings a matter to our attention that tears at our hearts, maybe even brings us to our knees. But then, sadly, so often that is all that happens. Although it consumes us for a little while and we can't

These children now have hope.

stop thinking about it, eventually we start to explore something else and forget.

Because we see and hear so much nowadays, soon our hearts stop hurting. We get used to things as they are.

But that is not the way of Jesus.

Christ was the One who saw the multitudes and wept.

So many times as I learn and relearn the reality these children face, I again realize that for too long I missed something important. So I cry out, "Lord, what is wrong with me? How could I possibly forget?"

I get so caught up in my day-to-day activities that weeks and months and even years pass, and I don't realize how quickly they have gone.

Please don't get so involved in today's trivia that you forget eternity awaits us all. Keep in mind those who are captive in the worst sort of prisons because, "I tell you the truth, whatever you did for one of the least of these brothers of mine, you did for me" (Matthew 25:40). The opposite is also true: "Whatever you did not do for one of the least of these, you did not do for me" (Matthew 25:45).

It is for Jesus' sake that we act. It is in His name that we sacrifice.

Together, you and I, we can make dreams come true for precious children. We can and we must.

One of the earlier memories of my college days in the United States is about a television show starring George Burns. He looked old, really old. He wore these round glasses like Gandhi, whom I respect so much. He was always puffing a cigar in between his stories and songs.

There was something about him that I just liked. One thing was this song he sang, and he did it often. A few words really stuck with me, "I wish I was 18 again." (You can probably hear it on YouTube.)[3]

When the Lord called me to serve Him, I was barely 16! I was living in a tiny village in a small state at the southern tip of India. Today, as I am writing these lines, I am 60! And I think to myself, "Whatever happened to time?" It kind of feels like it was yesterday when I left my home, traveling 2,000 miles to northern India to serve the Lord.

How did time slip by so fast . . . I don't know!

Along with George Burns, I too feel like singing, "I wish I

was 18 again." Why? Because there is so much to be done. The world is broken, filled with so much suffering, so many precious children—all lost and helpless. I want to lead them to Jesus, the One who is their hope.

But I can't turn back the clock. Time flies by and before we know it, it's all over. There's the final good-bye from this earth and to all the things we thought were so important and held on to so tightly.

Think about it! One hundred years from now, what do they matter? The house, cars, clothes, pearls, bank accounts, vacations, real estate, opinions of others, honors we sought and lived for. Oh, how silly we are not to live in the light of eternity!

Now is our time to see these precious people come to know God's love. Amy Carmichael once said, "We shall have all eternity to celebrate the victories, but we have only the few hours before sunset in which to win them."[4]

What a day it is going to be when we stand before the throne to find multitudes that no man can number from every nation, every tribe and every tongue! Our willingness to work these few hours will make eternity that much richer.

I plead with you to stop and think about what I am saying. Take your ID card or your driver's license out and look at it. See your date of birth on it. How old are you now? Maybe 20, 40, 60 years—you know how old you are. Add 100 years to your present age. Where are you now? Where is your house? How much do the opinions of others matter to you?

You see what I am talking about.

Live in the light of eternity. Love God by loving others. Make your life count.

Do you share a
🎀 **birthday**
with a child in Asia?

GFA-supported Bridge of Hope gives more than 75,000 destitute children the hope of a better future by providing the opportunity for an education, daily nutritious meals, medical attention, and the chance to experience the love of Jesus.

Find a little girl or boy who shares a birthday with you or a loved one, and decide to sponsor today.

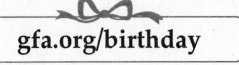

gfa.org/birthday

Or sponsor by contacting the GFA organization nearest you (see Appendix III).

FREQUENTLY ASKED QUESTIONS

I would like to be able to sit down with you and answer any questions that may have come up as you've read this book or discuss the plight of children in our generation. Who knows, maybe someday we will have such an opportunity. Until then, here are some questions people often ask—with their corresponding answers. You are always welcome to call or email our various national offices where we have people who can speak to the specific questions you may have.

I WANT TO GET INVOLVED. WHAT DO I DO?

Wonderful! I am glad the Lord has touched your heart with His concerns.

To sponsor a child through GFA's Bridge of Hope Program, mail in the preaddressed card included in this book, visit www.gfa.org/slumdog or contact the organization nearest you. (See Appendix III.)

For each $35 pledge you make, you will receive a packet that will include a photo and personal information of a child you can pray for, personally write to and build a lasting relationship with. You can make your donation monthly by check or money order, or you can set up automatic withdrawals, a method that saves on the cost of paper and staffing needs.

As soon as you receive your packet, or even before then, start to pray for your child and your child's family. The letter-writing kit that comes with the packet will enable you to begin writing to your child, who will write back to you on a regular basis.

How can I pray for needy children in this world and for the Dalits?

My belief is that prayer is the most effective tool God has given us and is truly a means to change the world. As the Lord burdens your heart for needy Dalit children, remember that one of the main reasons why these people stay in bondage is the belief that this life is simply their lot. Pray for them to realize their great worth in God's eyes.

Pray for health and safety. God knows those in need and can provide for them as we ask Him.

Pray that the Lord will raise up more Bridge of Hope centers to benefit these children, their families and their communities. Pray for all people's hearts to be open to Christ's love. In every Bridge of Hope center, each child has the opportunity to hear and understand how treasured he or she is in God's eyes.

Pray for your child's adjustment to the Bridge of Hope center. For many of the children, this is the first time they've ever attended school.

Pray for a supportive family and community. The initial response from parents could be negative, but over time, most fathers and mothers usually express sincere gratitude.

Pray for the Lord's will to be accomplished in each of these lives and that they will become an instrument of blessings to many.

Pray for a spiritual breakthrough all across Asia.

Be convinced that these children and the Dalits are on God's heart and that He is ready to answer our prayers if we but ask Him.

HOW DOES BRIDGE OF HOPE CHOOSE WHICH CHILDREN TO ENROLL?

One of the hardest things to witness is the large number of little boys and girls looking into a Bridge of Hope center, wanting to be involved but unable to join.

Selection is primarily based on the needs of the children and the prayers of the staff members. It is a painful process, but the staff at the centers, in partnership with the pastors of the local fellowships, pray through the needs of the children and the community. They reach out to all they can.

The hardest part is seeing children suffer without firsthand contact with the love of the Lord. Honestly, there are so many children out there who need help. One of the biggest requests from leaders on the mission field is, "Can we please open up more centers? There are so many children here who need our help."

As Bridge of Hope has the resources, more centers can be opened. But there are so many times that these leaders need to wait for the funding.

WHAT IS A TYPICAL DAY LIKE FOR A BRIDGE OF HOPE CHILD?

Monday through Friday, the children attend a government school for part of the day and then come to the Bridge of Hope center for several hours. The program has a holistic approach. Instead of focusing entirely on increasing the knowledge of the children or simply improving their physical health, Bridge of Hope invests in their overall development.

The tutors and staff help students individually with the subjects they were taught in school. There are opportunities for them to practice their mathematics, science and arts. Reading and writing are two major skills every child learns through GFA's Bridge of Hope Program. These are fundamental to liberating them from the cycle of poverty they have been trapped in all of their lives.

With guidance from the staff, these children start to excel in their studies. Each one performs better once they receive this personal love and assistance from the staff.

Students also develop social skills in this safe atmosphere as they watch leaders set a good example. They play games and sports to help them learn teamwork, respect, good manners and how to cooperate with one another. They discover that they are all equally loved and cared for by God.

Every day, Bridge of Hope children have the opportunity to experience Jesus' love. There are times of singing action songs and learning Bible stories such as when David slew Goliath, when Moses led the people of Israel across the Red Sea or when God created Adam and Eve.

Then every week, they learn something about how to take care of their bodies. These are simple practices such as brushing their hair and trimming their nails. Also provided for them every day is a nutritious meal, something many of the children will not have waiting for them at home. Vitamins are distributed, as they are needed, to keep the children healthy and to prevent problems such as blindness caused by a vitamin A deficiency. New school supplies and personal care items are handed out periodically, along with uniforms and books.

Each day is a special day for the children enrolled in Bridge of Hope. For most of them, this is the only place they will ever get the chance to just be a kid!

The goal of GFA's Bridge of Hope Program is to assist children to grow into godly individuals who will make a positive impact on their society. We want to give them the opportunity to become doctors, government officials, firemen, engineers, teachers, pastors, business leaders and godly parents. It is our hope that each of these children will become a responsible citizen, filled with the grace and love of the Lord and eager to be a light throughout their communities.

HOW DOES A BRIDGE OF HOPE CENTER BENEFIT A COMMUNITY?

Individually, the children are beacons of hope for their families, friends and communities. Their behaviors are changed through Bridge of Hope once they realize they have value in the eyes of the Lord. Soon they grow in newness of life. They stop stealing, cursing and running amok, instead becoming decent and respectful children. Time and time again, we hear how the change in these little ones affects the hearts of their parents.

As a whole, each Bridge of Hope center acts as a nexus for community activity. The children put on an annual Christmas program. They invite people to celebrate Children's Day, Parent's Day and other holidays. Their obvious joy and enthusiasm draw many townsfolk to the center to observe what is going on.

There are special community health sessions, teaching about such matters as brushing teeth and preventing AIDS. Counseling is available, and the staff visits the homes to minister to and pray for parents. There are literacy classes and vocational training where people can learn such skills as how to sew or fish.

A Bridge of Hope center transforms a community. Not only does the center reach out to the needs of the community, but the children are also making a difference by telling others what they have learned. They touch and change the lives around them and are a light that shines forth quite brilliantly!

A Bridge of Hope center brings hope to the entire community, helping to break the cycle of poverty and show people just how much the Lord loves them.

What makes GFA's Bridge of Hope Program unique?

The children sponsored through GFA's Bridge of Hope Program have the opportunity to be transformed, not only because of the physical means of food, clothing and a practical education, including the amazing blessing of being able to read the written word, but also through God's love. Although we are committed to alleviating the pains of this present world through physical aid and education, we also care about the spiritual condition of these precious children.

GFA's Bridge of Hope Program is a natural extension of our desire to bring hope through the love of God. Literally tens of thousands of children are experiencing a new life, but this is just the beginning.

There are still millions of children who are eagerly waiting for hope and an education. And it's our heart's desire to reach them, not only with the promise that education brings, but also with the love of Christ.

How does my monthly gift provide for children enrolled in Bridge of Hope?

Your donation to GFA's Bridge of Hope Program makes it possible for Bridge of Hope to provide life-changing assistance to your sponsored child, as well as thousands of children throughout Asia. Bridge of Hope provides children with an education and personal help with their studies; it also gives them school supplies such as books and backpacks as well as a clean and sturdy uniform to wear. Children receive practical items like towels and toothpaste. Each day they are served a nutritious meal, and every year there is a medical checkup with a trained doctor. Most important, this child will experience the love of the Living God through the prayers and care of Bridge of Hope staff.

There is much more to educating children than simply filling their heads with facts and figures. The staff knows how important it is that the students understand they are not doomed to the same fate as their parents and grandparents, and that they discover the true source of hope who can literally change the world in which they live.

As a sponsor of a Bridge of Hope child, what should I expect?

In the mail, you will receive a photo and information packet about your child, which will help you know how to pray for him or her. As a sponsor, you will have the incredible blessing of being able to pray for and build a lasting relationship with a specific child on the other side of the world. Though you may never meet this child, we believe the impact your prayers will have on this child and his or her family will truly change their lives.

Your role is a vital one. Your financial support helps provide for a valuable education and lays the foundation for a future of promise. Your ongoing prayers for your sponsored child are another investment that has the potential to bear eternal rewards—not only in one child's heart but also in their family and community.

Your child will be praying for you as well, because you will become special to him or her and to the family. Many parents of Bridge of Hope children have a hard time fully understanding why a stranger on the other side of the world would want to send their child to school, feed them a daily meal and buy them a uniform. Your giving will help provide these families opportunities to understand Christ's love.

Your family can be changed through sponsorship, too. Many sponsors find it an excellent way to bond as a family.

You may never know the full effect of your support, because when you make a difference in the life of a child, your impact never really ends.

DO I NEED TO COMMIT TO SPONSORING FOR A CERTAIN LENGTH OF TIME?

Although we give sponsors the opportunity to support children throughout their entire education, no time commitment is required.

We are convinced of the Lord's sovereignty, deep love and abundant provision for all these children. Depending on individual situations, some supporters may desire to assist their sponsored child for the entire length of his or her education, while others choose to do so for only a year or two. We understand that your circumstances could change. You may discontinue your sponsorship at any time.

HOW CAN I GET TO KNOW MY SPONSORED CHILD BETTER?

There are several ways to learn more about your child, the country they live in and the Bridge of Hope ministry.

1. Read the articles on our website, www.gfa.org/slumdog, in our emails and in our literature that highlight news about Bridge of Hope programs across Asia. These articles spotlight children whose lives, families and communities have been changed through their encounters with God and His love.

2. We highly recommend the book *Operation World* by Jason Mandryk as a helpful resource for understanding both the culture and prayer needs of the nation in which your sponsored child lives. More information is available at www.operationworld.org.

3. You may write to your child and receive letters in return. Here are several examples of letters from children:

Dear Rachael Smith,
    Hello.
    Hello, Rachael, how are you? I am fine. I am very happy to getting your letter. Thank you very-very much for all you have send me. Thank you for the beautiful pictures you send me. How lovely these are, God will bless. I agree with you that you and me are friends. Now you are my best friend. I am very thankful to God so that He will met you to me. I am very lucky that you are my friend. Thank you for your wish of Birthday. I enjoyed my birthday. Again I want to thank you for all you have send me. God will help you. God is great.
    Thanking you, with prayers,
    Yours lovingly,
    Danvir (12)

Dear Nathan and Olivia White,

Hello.

Praise the Lord. How are you? I hope you will be fine. I am fine and my family is doing well. I am going school for getting good education. My teachers are very kind and always helps us. I learned many good things in school. Thank you for writing me letter. I am always waiting for your letter. Always you inspired me for God's greatness. I love you people because you believe in God. I also believe in God very much. God will be help for you. Thanking you please keep pray for me.

Thanking you with prayers,

Yours lovingly,

Lomash (11)

Dear Miss Kiersten Oliver,

How are you? Warmest greetings to you in the name of Jesus. By the grace of God, I am safe. Hoping you are also same.

By the love you are showing, I am able to go to school regularly and study well. We are benefited in many ways by the Bridge of Hope, such as getting Education, learning, Bible stories and verses, participating in weekly contest quiz games etc. I am also attending to the Sunday school.

These two months we got away-rains, all the rivers over flowing. The lower places are flooded. Many people lost their lives. Some lost their homes. Many are suffering with different problems. Please pray for our state.

In the project center we are taught how to pray in the morning, evening and at the time of study, meals etc. We are getting healthy food in the project. I thank God a lot. Please pray for me. I do pray for you.

Yours lovingly,
Rahdak (11)

Corresponding with your sponsored child not only strengthens your relationship, but also will be a great encouragement to a child living in difficult circumstances. You can personally write to your child using the special stationery and envelopes GFA provides. Your initial letter-writing material will be included in your sponsorship packet.

WHAT IS THE MINISTRY OF GFA?

GFA is a nonprofit organization deeply committed to seeing communities transformed through the love of Christ demonstrated in word and deed.

We focus on serving the neediest nations and communities. We are a bridge between people in situations and countries that are more well-off and people who are helpless and suffering in our world.

GFA comes alongside thousands of well-trained national workers and supports them through prayer and assistance as they bring hope to the most needy. We are engaged in dozens of projects, such as caring for poor children, slum dwellers and widows and orphans; providing clean water by funding wells; supporting medical missions; and meeting the needs of those in leprosy colonies.

$\mathcal{B}$ELIEVE IT OR $\mathcal{N}$OT

THE 4/14 WINDOW are children between the ages of 4 and 14. These are the critical years when a child's character and worldview are molded.[1]

➤ 1.2 billion children worldwide are in the 4/14 Window.[2]

➤ More than 300 million children—one-fourth of the entire 4/14 Window—live in the South Asian countries of India, Bangladesh, Myanmar, Nepal and Sri Lanka.[3]

➤ If these South Asian children formed their own nation, its population would be as large as the United States.

CHILD LABOR standards have been established by the United Nations to protect children from exploitation in the workplace.

➤ 150 million of the 4/14 Window are child laborers, employed in violation of these standards.[4]

➤ 60 percent of these child laborers are 11 years or younger.[5]

➤ More than 50 million children are in "hazardous work" involving long hours; physical, psychological or sexual abuse; or dangerous equipment, confined spaces or toxic environments.[6]

HUMAN TRAFFICKING is one of the fastest-growing criminal enterprises in the world today, soon to surpass the drug trade.

➤ 2.5 million people around the world are in forced labor at any given time as a result of trafficking.[7]

➤ More than half of trafficking victims are from Asia and the Pacific.[8]

➤ Every year, an estimated 1.2 million children become victims of trafficking.[9]

- Nepali women and girls, some as young as 9 years old, are sold into India's red-light district—10,000 to 15,000 per year.[10]

- Sri Lanka is touted as a pedophile's paradise, with up to 40,000 child prostitutes—mostly boys—trafficked to serve tourists.[11]

- 300,000 children worldwide are currently trafficked as child soldiers.[12]

IMPROVED SANITATION FACILITIES are available for only about one out of three people in India.[13]

➤ That means that up to 800 million people use public or private latrines that must be cleaned by "manual scavengers."

➤ This is the job of more than a million Dalits in India.[14]

Contact Information

For more information contact the organization nearest you.

Australia: GFA Australia Inc.
PO Box 3587
Toowoomba QLD 4350
Freephone: 1300 889 339
info@gospelforasia.org.au

Canada: GFA
245 King Street E
Stoney Creek, ON L8G 1L9
Toll-free: 1-888-WIN-ASIA
info@gfa.ca

Finland: GFA Finland ry
PL 63, 65101 Vaasa, Finland
Phone: 050 036 9699
infofi@gfa.org

Korea: 아시아복음선교회 한국지부
(GFA Korea)
Seok-Am Blg 5th floor
6-9 Tereran-ro 25 gil
Yeoksam-dong, Gangnam-gu
Seoul 135-080
Toll-free: (080) 801-0191
infokorea@gfa.org.kr

(more offices on next page)

NEW ZEALAND: GFA
                       PO Box 302580
                       North Harbour
                       Auckland 0751
                       Toll-free: 0800-819-819
                       infonz@gfa.org

SOUTH AFRICA: GFA (SA)
                       P.O. Box 28880
                       Sunridge Park
                       Port Elizabeth 6008
                       Phone: 041 360-0198
                       infoza@gfa.org

UNITED KINGDOM: GFA (U.K.)
                       PO Box 316
                       Manchester M22 2DJ
                       Phone: 0161 946 9484
                       infouk@gfa.org

UNITED STATES: GFA, Inc.
                       1116 St. Thomas Way
                       Wills Point, TX 75169
                       Toll-free: 1-800-WIN-ASIA
                       info@gfa.org

If you have been blessed by this book,
I would really like to hear from you.
Please send me an email at kp@gfa.org.

Notes

INTRODUCTION

1. *Slumdog Millionaire*. DVD. Directed by Danny Boyle. 2009. Christian Colson.

2. Jason Mandryk, *Operation World: 7th edition* (Colorado Springs, CO: Biblica, 2010), p. 410.

3. Luis Bush, "The 4-14 Window – 'The Core of the Core,'" *4-14 Window Global Initiative* (http://4to14window. com/4-14-window-core-core). (Accessed March 21, 2011).

4. Mandryk, *Operation World,* p. 432.

CHAPTER 1: STOLEN CHILDHOOD

1. Daniel Berrigan, "Communion," *inward/outward: A Project of the Church of the Saviour* (http://www.inwardoutward. org/author/daniel-berrigan). (Accessed March 21, 2011).

2. UNICEF, *The State of the World's Children: 2005* (http:// www.unicef.org/sowc05/english/sowc05_chapters.pdf). (Accessed March 24, 2011).

3. Mandryk, *Operation World,* p. 410.

4. Ibid., p. 410.

5. Ibid., p. 445.

6. Chris Morris, "Diet of Mud and Despair in Indian Village," *BBC News* (http://news.bbc.co.uk/2/hi/8682558.stm). (Accessed March 21, 2011).

7. Yacouba Diallo et al., *Global Child Labour Developments: Measuring Trends from 2004 to 2008* (Geneva: International Labour Office, 2010), p. 10.

8. UNICEF, *The State of the World's Children: Special Edition* (New York, NY: UNICEF, 2009), p. 24.

9. Megha Bahree, "Child Labor," *Forbes.com* (http://www.forbes.com/forbes/2008/0225/072.html). (Accessed March 21, 2011).

10. Ibid.

11. Joseph D'souza, *Dalit Freedom: Now and Forever* (Centennial, CO: Dalit Freedom Network, 2004), p. 42.

12. Mandryk, *Operation World*, p. 410.

13. "Child Labour," *Aide Internationale pour l'enfance* (http://www.aipe-cci.org/en/child-labor/en-enfants-travail.html). (Accessed March 21, 2011).

CHAPTER 2: ONCE A SLUMDOG, ALWAYS A SLUMDOG

1. Mother Teresa, *Where There Is Love, There Is God: A Path to Closer Union with God and Greater Love* (New York, NY: Doubleday Religion, 2010), p. 82.

2. "Advocating the Rights of the Marginalised for Justice and Equality," *Dalit Solidarity* (http://www.dalitsolidarity.org/). (Accessed March 21, 2011).

3. "Dalits fined for daring to drink water from tap," *Dalit Freedom Network* (http://www.dalitnetwork.org/go?/dfn/news/2010/10/). (Accessed March 21, 2011).

4. K.P. Yohannan, "I Am Nobody."

5. K.P. Yohannan, "Vendor of Sticks."

6. "Dalit beaten to death in Uttar Pradesh," *Thaindian News* (http://www.thaindian.com/newsportal/uncategorized/dalit-beaten-to-death-in-uttar-pradesh_100205461.html). (Accessed March 21, 2011).

7. Mandryk, *Operation World,* p. 408.

8. D'souza, *Dalit Freedom,* p. 37.

9. National Sample Survey Organization, Ministry of Statistics and Programme Implementation, Government of India, *Employment and Unemployment Situation Among Social Groups in India 2004–05: NSS 61st Round (July 2004–June 2005),* Report No. 516, October 2006, pp. 21–22.

CHAPTER 3: OPEN YOUR EYES

1. John Cook, comp., *The Book of Positive Quotations,* 2nd ed., ed.Steve Deger and Leslie Ann Gibson (Minneapolis, MN: Fairview Press), p. 112.

CHAPTER 4: WINDS OF CHANGE

1. Martin Luther King Jr. "I've Been to the Mountain Top" (speech, Mason Temple, Memphis, TN, April 3, 1968).

2. "Discrimination: Briefing on Dalit and the Caste System," *Child Rights Information Network* (http://www.crin. org/resources/infoDetail.asp?ID=20802&flag=report). (Accessed March 21, 2011).

3. "Poor mothers set up 'kid bazaar,' " *The Telegraph* (http://www.telegraphindia.com/1110108/jsp/siliguri/ story_13407595.jsp). (Accessed March 21, 2011).

CHAPTER 5: IT IS HAPPENING

1. William Shakespeare, *The Merchant of Venice* (New York, NY: Washington Square Press, 1992).

2. "2004: Thousands die in Asian tsunami," *BBC* (http:// news.bbc.co.uk/onthisday/hi/dates/stories/december/26/ newsid_4631000/4631713.stm). (Accessed March 21, 2011).

CHAPTER 6: WHAT NOW?

1. James R. Lowell, *The Writings of James Russell Lowell in Prose and Poetry* (James Russell Lowell, 1870), p. 243.

2. UNICEF, *The State of the World's Children: Special Edition,* p. 25.

3. Steven Curtis Chapman, "What Now," Copyright © September 21, 2004, Sparrow Records (adm. Worldwide by EMI CMG Publishing). All rights reserved.

4. E.M. Bounds, *Power Through Prayer* (Radford, VA: Wilder Publications, 2008), p. 15.

Chapter 7: Make Your Life Count

1. Linda Picone, *The Daily Book of Positive Quotations* (Minneapolis, MN: Fairview Press, 2008), p. 163.

2. C.S. Lewis, *The Screwtape Letters* (New York, NY: Macmillan, 1982), p. 61. (paraphrased)

3. 2007. *George Burns–I Wish I Was Eighteen Again* [Video], Retrieved February 3, 2011, from http://www.youtube.com/watch?v=F3c-WBn5cCg. (Accessed March 21, 2011).

4. Amy Carmichael, *Things as They Are: Mission Work in Southern India* (Princeton, NJ: Princeton University, 1906), p. 158.

Appendix II: Believe It or Not

1. The United Nations statistics cited in this book cover the 10-year age range from 5 to 14.

2. Diallo et al., *Global Child Labour Developments: Measuring Trends from 2004 to 2008,* p. 10.

3. Estimated by combining statistics on the "Under 15" population from *2010 World Population Data Sheet* (Washington, D.C.: Population Reference Bureau, 2010), pp. 6–9 with statistics on the "Under 5" population from *The State of the World's Children, Special Edition: Statistical Tables* (New York: UNICEF, 2009), pp. 28–31.

4. Diallo et al., *Global Child Labour Developments: Measuring Trends from 2004 to 2008,* p. 10.

5. Ibid., p. 10.

6. Ibid., p. 10.

7. United Nations Office on Drugs and Crime, *Human Trafficking FAQs* (http://www.unodc.org/unodc/en/human-trafficking/faqs.html). (Accessed March 21, 2011).

8. United Nations Global Initiative to Fight Human Trafficking, *Human Trafficking: The Facts* (http://www.unglobalcompact.org/docs/issues_doc/labour/Forced_labour/HUMAN_TRAFFICKING_-_THE_FACTS_-_final.pdf). (Accessed March 21, 2011).

9. UNICEF, *Child Protection Information Sheet: Trafficking* (http://www.unicef.org/protection/files/trafficking.pdf). (Accessed March 21, 2011).

10. U.S. Department of State, *Trafficking in Persons Report 2009*, p. 217 (http://www.state.gov/documents/organization/123357.pdf). (Accessed March 21, 2011).

11. International Labour Organization, *Anti-Child Trafficking Legislation in Asia: A Six-Country Review*, 2006, p. 70 (http://www.ilo.org/wcmsp5/groups/public/---asia/---ro-bangkok/documents/publication/wcms_bk_pb_76_en.pdf). (Accessed March 21, 2011).

12. UNICEF, *Children in Conflict and Emergencies* (http://www.unicef.org/protection/index_armedconflict.html). (Accessed March 21, 2011).

13. *2010 World Population Data Sheet*, p. 16. An improved sanitation facility is one that hygienically separates sewage from human contact.

14. CHR&GJ and Human Rights Watch, *On the Margins of Profit: Rights at Risk in the Global Economy*, vol. 20, no. 3(G), February 2008, p. 31 (http://www.hrw.org/sites/default/files/reports/bhr0208_1.pdf). (Accessed March 21, 2011).

Free Book!

Many people have said this book changed their life.

Get your **free** copy of K.P. Yohannan's book *Revolution in World Missions*. It might change your life too!

"Other than the Holy Bible, no other book has challenged and been used to change my life and thinking. . ."
—*Francis, TX*

"It's a must read!"
—*Gladys, TX*

"It changed my life."
—*Emily, IN*

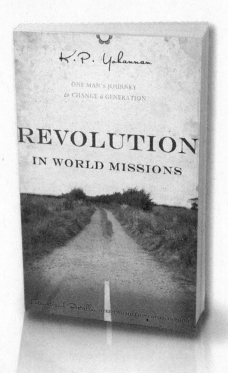

More than 3.9 million copies in print!

Be Encouraged by What God Is Doing in Asia!

FREE EMAIL UPDATES

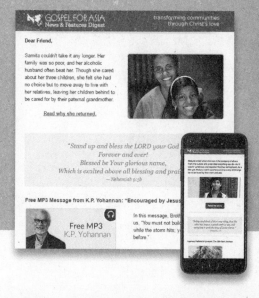

Get GFA's weekly email digest, filled with photos, videos, stories and news from the mission field. You're sure to be encouraged and inspired!

"I love reading the GFA emails to my kids and praying for the missionaries." —Theresa, MN

"Thank you for your emails with stories of hope." —Richard, GA

Start getting these updates—sign up today!

gfa.org/email

Don't worry! GFA will not sell, lease or trade your personal information. You can opt out of receiving these free emails at any time.

Free E-books and Messages!

MP3s

E-books

Get access to Dr. K.P. Yohannan's entire collection of downloadable e-books and messages—**more than 100 FREE resources!** Includes:

- *Against the Wind*
- *Destined to Soar*
- *Living in the Light of Eternity*
- *The Road to Reality*
- *Touching Godliness*

and many, many more!

You can also download e-books by Dr. K.P.'s wife, Gisela—also free!

- *Broken for a Purpose*
- *Consider Your Call*
- *Dear Sister*
- *Let Me Walk with You*

>>>>>> **gfa.org/FreeResources** >>>>>>

You may also purchase physical copies of the books and booklets by contacting the GFA organization nearest you (see Appendix III).

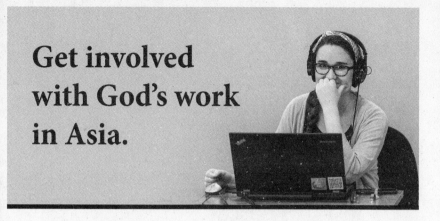

Get involved with God's work in Asia.

Your life can expand the work of national missionaries when you serve behind the scenes.

Become a GFA Volunteer
- Share the ministry with others through social media and blogs.
- Hand out free books to challenge and inspire friends and family.
- Represent GFA at local events. (We'll train and equip you!)

Serve in a College Internship
- Gain work experience and grow spiritually, too.
- Programs are available for a range of majors.
- Internships may qualify for college credit.

Join GFA's Home Team Staff
- Serve behind the scenes to send Christ's love across the globe.
- Be part of a community that pursues Christ passionately in prayer and worship.
- Servant-hearted people with a variety of skills—from network administration to building maintenance—are needed.

Learn more about how you can get involved.
gfa.org/yourlife

GFA's School of Discipleship

Encounter God | Know Him More

Your life will never be the same.

You will:

Transform the lives of Asia's hurting and oppressed by serving at GFA's U.S. home office.

Learn to embrace spiritual disciplines through prayer, solitude and devotions.

Grow spiritually through classes that emphasize real-life application of God's Word.

Live a simple lifestyle focused on knowing Christ and making Him known.

Can you die to yourself for one year?

Learn more and get your free information kit.
gfa.org/OneYearSchool

School of Discipleship is open to dedicated Christian single adults ages 18-27.

 /gfaschool • gfaschool • disciple365.org • /gfaschool • @gfaschool

"I have never seen deeper growth in my life than during my time here."—Jordan